MERMAIDS and MAGIC SHOWS

MERMAIDS
and
MAGIC SHOWS

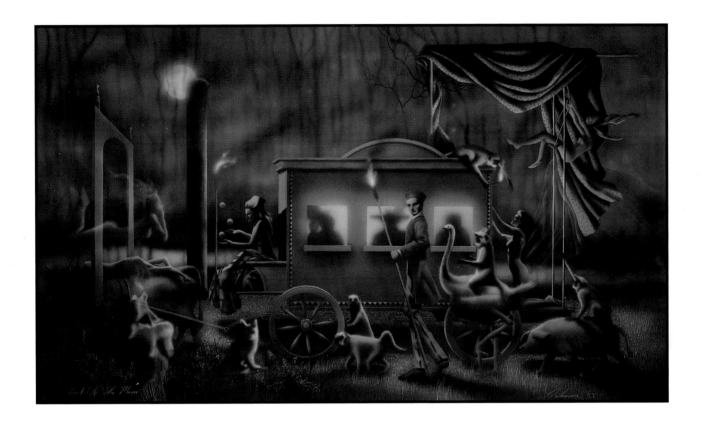

THE PAINTINGS OF
DAVID DELAMARE

TEXT BY
NIGEL SUCKLING

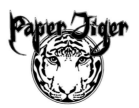

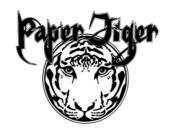

An imprint of Dragon's World Ltd
Limpsfield
Surrey RH8 0DY
Great Britain

First published by Dragon's World 1994

Editor: Fiona Trent
Design: Cooper Wilson
Editorial Director: Pippa Rubinstein

The catalogue record for this book is available from the British Library

ISBN 1 85028 249 8

Printed in Singapore

CONTENTS

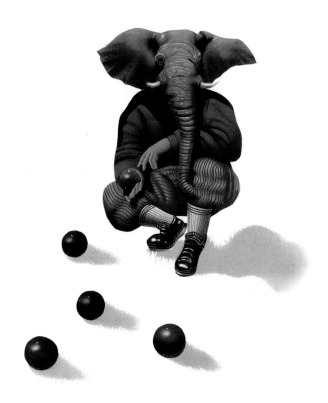

INTRODUCTION

David Delamare was born in Leicester, England, where he lived until about three years of age, when his family moved to the United States. An only child, his parents first met during World War II. His father was a paratrooper from Portland, so his English mother was, in effect, a GI bride, though it was some years before she was convinced that Oregon was where she wanted to live. However, she came to like it, perhaps because the weather is similar to Britain's, and has remained ever since.

The state offers a great variety of landscapes, ranging from spectacular scenery on the Pacific coast to snowy mountains inland to desert in the south. The city of Portland is also quite attractive, being large enough to feel urban without losing the quality of being a neighbourhood. It has also remained David Delamare's base and he is very happy with the rather Bohemian area where he lives and works. It has a wide variety of restaurants, cinemas, galleries and live theatre venues, all within walking distance, which is useful because Delamare does not drive. After a long debate about whether he should keep his private life and work separate, he decided they should be integrated, so he basically lives in his studio and enjoys always having his work close at hand.

After graduating from Portland State University in 1978 with a degree in fine arts, graphic arts and printmaking, he spent a year as Artist in Residence at Marshall High School, leaving with the impression that, however much he loved art, teaching it was not for him. A subsequent stint confirmed this lesson and he has since turned down offers to teach.

Delamare left college determined to make a living as some kind of artist; the issue was 'How'? An arts degree is not like one in accountancy, for example, and waving it about does not open many doors. He could see no path, just a huge art arena with no clear rules on how to go about making any money in it. What he did do in 1980 was open a graphics studio with a partner; they were prepared to take on any work that could be squeezed into the category of 'graphics' provided it paid the rent and food bills. Much of it turned out to be lettering for shop windows and signs, but gradually the range of commissions broadened and snowballed. 'Cracks of opportunity to do more creative things began to spring open. For example, a commission from a record store for a picture of Charlie Parker led to more and more requests for paintings till signage became subordinate.'

Around the same time Delamare discovered galleries as a viable outlet for his work, and eventually, in 1983, the Whole Image Studio sign was taken down and replaced with his own name. Delamare has since survived by doing what he loves most – a happy position which he attributes to the lucky breaks that have helped shape his career so far.

Launching out on his own was scary and not without trauma: 'Looking back, it's hard to see the point at which work went from being sporadic to busy. There were many dry periods when I wondered how to pay the rent, but somehow the flow became steady.' He still finds, though, that when people ask what he does and the reply is 'artist', they tend to say, 'But what do you do for a living?'

One trauma he could have done without in those early days was the burning down of his studio, which destroyed a large collection of pictures. Since the fire he has kept transparencies of all his work in a safe deposit box elsewhere. In a curious way one of the most depressing things about the fire was that it did not burn the place totally to the ground. Seeing the charred remains of cherished objects in the wreckage was somehow worse for Delamare than if they had been reduced to ashes. Did it shift his perception of life? 'Maybe a bit. A darker element perhaps came in – a feeling of never knowing when a brick is going to fall on you. I was probably more precious about my pictures before the fire. Now it feels fine that someone else has them. When I have had my own time with a painting I don't need it on my wall. I am more sentimental about other things, such as train or theatre tickets, which are catalysts for memory.' He enjoys seeing his pictures in settings and frames that he probably would not have chosen.

Although he has moved around the building, Delamare still lives in the eighty-year-old block where the fire took place. The neighbourhood has grown more 'desirable' since he moved in, when the bookshop downstairs was a bar used by motorcycle gangs. His neighbours were quite colourful then, too. This was literally true of the family next door who, from grandfather down to the children, were tattooed, the father being an ex-biker and carnival barker.

The area is tamer now, but has yet to show signs of becoming genteel, and Delamare has no plans to move. He likes city life. When he goes to the beach he cannot sleep for the first couple of nights because of the silence. He is by temperament more an observer of people than of nature and, as mentioned, if you are not a driver it helps to have your entertainment laid on within strolling distance.

Can he drive? 'I have never driven a car or had any inclination to learn. And I enjoy the different perspective this gives. I love trains and buses and the different types of people you see on them.'

There are several other things he has never done: he has never married, never owned a house and never felt any urge to have children. He does not believe in living life according to the expectations of others. He enjoys the fresh perspective that such slight displacement brings, and in his case it feeds back into his work.

The 'slight displacement' carries over into Delamare's sense of nationality. Although he left Britain as a child, he remains conscious of his Englishness and this shows in his work, particularly the anthropomorphic pieces, even when they do not have Stonehenge in the background. This may be due to the influence of his mother and grandmother, and helped by a steady two-way traffic of relatives across the Atlantic. On the other hand, it could be innate. Whatever the reason, when it comes to contrasting American and British views of life he usually finds himself leaning towards the latter.

For

instance,

in the USA

no great difference

is perceived between one's

public and private life, but in

Britain there is a strict demarcation

and a tradition of maintaining a

decorous front at all costs – a sort of

social game playing. Delamare believes this

encourages eccentricity (of which he naturally

approves) and perhaps also explains why the country pro-

duces so many great actors and spies. Game playing in a broader,

and not very serious, sense is also a very British thing, which crops up in many

Delamare paintings. He has visited Britain many times and feels very comfortable there – even down

to the 'rat-in-a-maze' quality of London streets, in which most Americans find it difficult to maintain

any sense of direction.

This clinging sense of Englishness is, he feels, probably quite useful: 'The virtue of feeling slightly dis-

placed is that you constantly have to assess what your position is.' Or to put it another way, originality

does not usually come about by pure chance. One cannot accept conventional views of life and still

expect to have anything original to say about it. It is often necessary to be detached from a situation in

order to appreciate it fully.

MERMAIDS

David Delamare's first mermaid picture was also one of his first pure painting commissions. It came in about 1980 when he was asked to do a mermaid mural to decorate the dining-room wall of Buttertoes, a newly opened restaurant in his native Portland. He was happy enough with the result, without in the least suspecting that it was the first step in a dramatic departure for his life and work.

A few weeks later an author, having seen the mural, came knocking on his door charged with the notion of jointly producing a lavishly illustrated book of lore and legend to be called *The Mermaid Chronicles*. As it turned out, the book never came to fruition, but it prompted Delamare over the next few years, and intermittently ever since, to produce a vast body of mermaid pictures. The popularity of these pictures launched him as an independent artist, and their impact on his own imagination turned him into a different kind of artist.

Mermaids have an enormous range of appeal as a theme, as demonstrated by their lasting popularity down the ages. This has survived despite a general acceptance over the past couple of centuries that these glamorous creatures almost certainly do not exist in reality. Mermaids have also survived Freud's deconstruction of the myth into a metaphor for rather dubious and misdirected sexual impulses. Freud had hardly done his damage, when mermaids defiantly resurfaced in the work of Surrealists, such as Paul Delvaux and René Magritte. They have continued to haunt the realms of art and entertainment ever since. We may know they do not exist in the real world, but some part of our collective psyche remains convinced that they ought to.

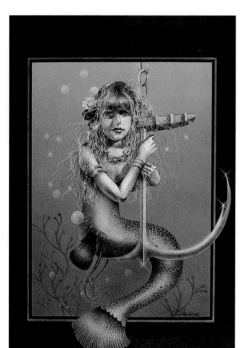

LITTLE MERMAID ON ANCHOR 1983
Gouache 12 x 16in (30 x 40cm)
Although not always possible, Delamare loves having real people pose for him. In this case the model was the daughter of the owner of the shop below his studio.

MERMAID EGGS 1981
Gouache 16 x 20in (40 x 50cm)
The whole area of birth is a cloudy one in mermaid lore, which gives a great deal of licence for artistic interpretation. Delamare's approach, however, does not aim to demystify the subject by too much pseudo-biological speculation, which he sees as missing the point. To him the metaphor that sustains the mermaid myth is that they represent a longing that cannot be consummated. The fascination of mermaids for men is more mystical than physical.

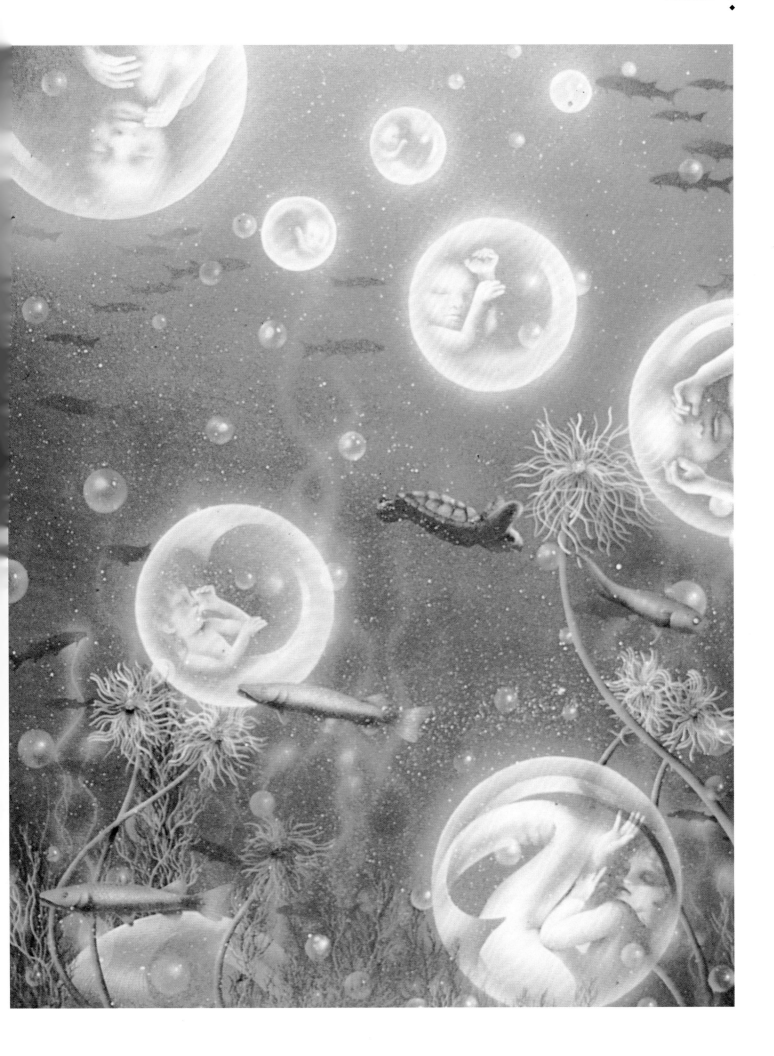

On a purely aesthetic level mermaids and their environs provide other attractions, as Delamare soon learned. For example, when doing a surface composition, the horizon provides a wonderfully graphic line for balancing a picture, while in underwater scenes the weightlessness of the subjects allows a tremendous fluidity of composition.

When painting mermaids Delamare prefers to work from live models. Does this ever lead to complications with his girlfriend? 'Not at all. She is probably more sane about it than I am. Besides, the psychology of working with models is less romantic than most people imagine.'

At college, Delamare confesses that he was as excited as all the other male students by the prospect of life classes and having an attractive young woman sit naked in their midst, but the reality turned out to be a rather clinical experience. After five minutes, licentiousness was the last thing on their minds.

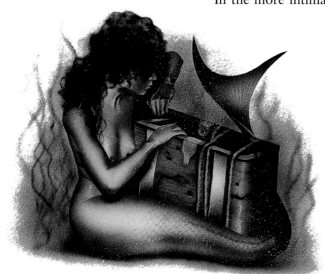

MERMAID WITH CHEST 1983
Pencil and ink 10 x 10in (25 x 25cm)

In the more intimate atmosphere of his own studio professional detachment is occasionally less concrete, but it remains the rule. 'It is funny how the parameters of propriety operate,' says Delamare. 'As long as the conversation stays on a professional level, talking about art in general or the subject in hand, everything is fine. Start chatting on a personal level and more orthodox conventions from the outside world creep in.'

The whole subject of art and nudity is riddled with such anomalies. Apparently, the film-maker Peter Greenaway has trouble with the release of his films in the United States because of their nude content. Greenaway himself sees the problem as simply a clash between the way he and the American film-going public 'read' nudity. For Greenaway it means no more or less than it does in classical paintings, whereas in the US cinema it is usually taken as a preamble to sex and/or violence.

Does Delamare use professional models? 'Never. This is crucial to my work because professional models come with preconceptions of how poses should look. Ideally, models should be friends. I enjoy taking aspects of their personality and incorporating them into the work, the challenge of depicting someone from more than just their appearance.'

When no friend is suitable for a conception he has in mind, Delamare may resort to scouring the streets for a suitable model. If he sees a stranger who fits the bill, he will try to get an introduction before asking them to pose. It helps that he is quite well known in the neighbourhood where he lives and works, so has a large pool of acquaintances to call on.

Casting the characters for a composition and then setting up his studio are things Delamare enjoys almost as much as painting itself – something he attributes to his frustrated desire to be a theatrical director. Seriously? 'Well, no. I love the theatre but it is probably not a serious ambition. I was recently offered the chance to do some set design, which could have been a way in. As a horizon-broadening experience I would have accepted, if the time sequence had been right, but I was also a bit intimidated. Theatre is a collaborative effort, decisions are made by committee. I value my independence as a painter.'

One advantage of that independence is being able to choose his working hours. Typical working days fall into two categories. If he has an ongoing project in hand, such as a book, he tends to work very steadily and intensely, and hardly dares to stop because if a fertile mood slips away it can be very difficult to start its flow again. Lurking at the back of his mind, with books, is always the fear of hitting a mental block and not being able to meet the schedule.

With single or more loosely connected pieces the pace is easier. Over the course of a week he often puts in the same number of hours, but irregularly. A fairly constant rule is that he never works in the morning.

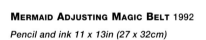

MERMAID ADJUSTING MAGIC BELT 1992
Pencil and ink 11 x 13in (27 x 32cm)

This touches on the whole subject of mermaids using some sort of talismanic device, such as a belt or cap, to capture the human object of their desire. By wearing it the human can enter the undersea world. Conversely, if a human can lure a mermaid out of the water and capture her magic comb or whatever, she is compelled to remain in a two-legged state.

Afternoons are for tasks that do not require too much inspiration, but twilight is the magic time because Delamare is by nature a night person. He loves its mystery and the feeling that life suddenly becomes more open to interpretation. With darkness his creativity starts flowing. A common work pattern is that once it is dark he works for a few hours, then goes out for a beer and a chat with friends, and returns to the studio for more work, sometimes till 2.30 or 3.00 a.m.

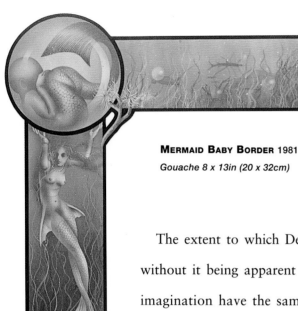

Mermaid Baby Border 1981
Gouache 8 x 13in (20 x 32cm)

When working on loose pieces Delamare never tries to force the pace. If he cannot get into the right frame of mind he just waits 'till the clouds part and the right mood comes'. Often he reaches a point of 'visual saturation', where he cannot judge whether a piece is finished or not, or even if it is any good, in which case the picture is put away till his objectivity returns.

The extent to which Delamare uses photography in his mermaid pictures varies greatly without it being apparent in the finished work. That is to say, those painted purely from imagination have the same degree of reality as those derived largely from photographs. Somewhere in between come the pictures which have been painted directly from models, with photographs being used merely as reference for lighting and mood. The chosen approach depends on the circumstances or the idea he has in mind, or whether it is realistic for the model to hold a particular pose for any length of time, given that his studio is unable to reproduce the weightlessness of a mermaid's natural habitat.

Any preparatory sketches are very rough and purely for the sake of establishing overall composition. He expands his sketches by hand and eye rather than using an overhead projector because the balance can usually be improved in the process. Geometric patterns quite often underlie Delamare's compositions, but they develop intuitively and not as a result of conscious deliberation.

When he began the series of mermaid pictures Delamare had no detailed scenario of the mer-world in his mind. It just developed as he went along, with each picture adding its bit. Many aspects of the mer-world remain obscure, such as the role and significance of mermen, but he is in no rush to unravel the secrets if it also means demystifying the subject. He is not interested in any rationalistic approach, that destroys what it seeks to examine.

When not simply celebrating the elusive beauty of mermaids, Delamare's pictures often explore their relationship with humans; the essence of which is that, being from an alien environment, mermaids represent an almost unattainable ideal of beauty, and any love for them is usually doomed, either to disappointment or enormous complication.

Tattooed Mermaid 1982
Gouache 16 x 20in (40 x 50cm)
The idea behind this picture was that the tattoos reflect the commerce between mermaids and sailors, though the question of which group might have originated the art remains unclear in Delamare's mind.

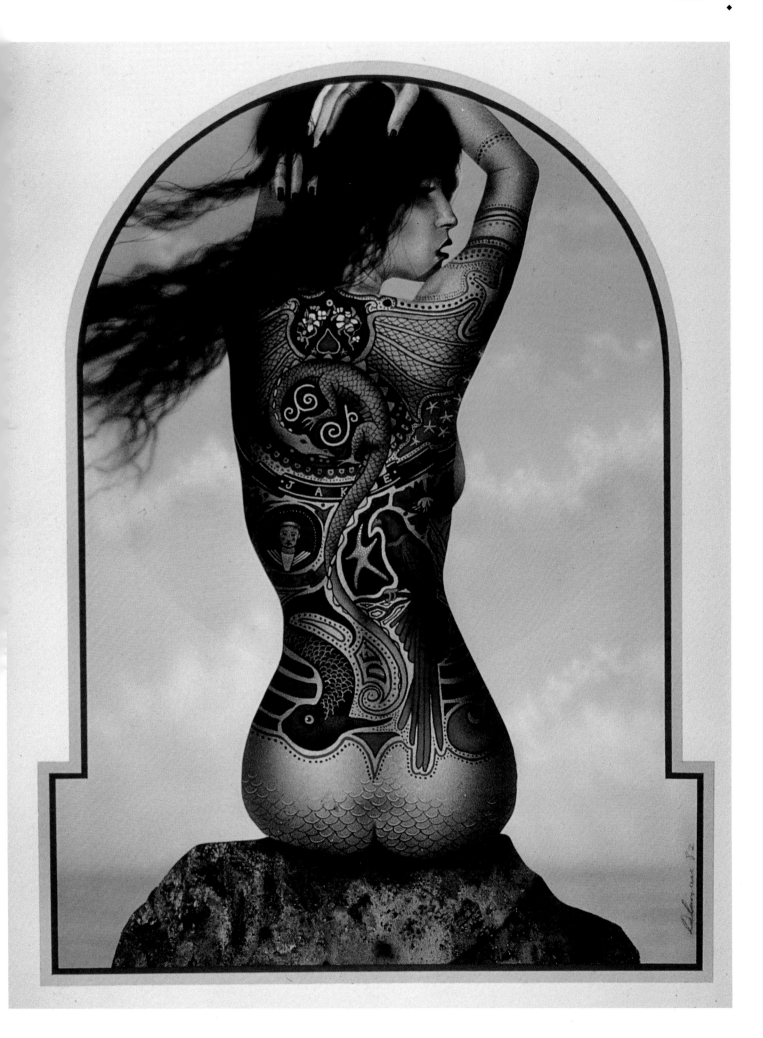

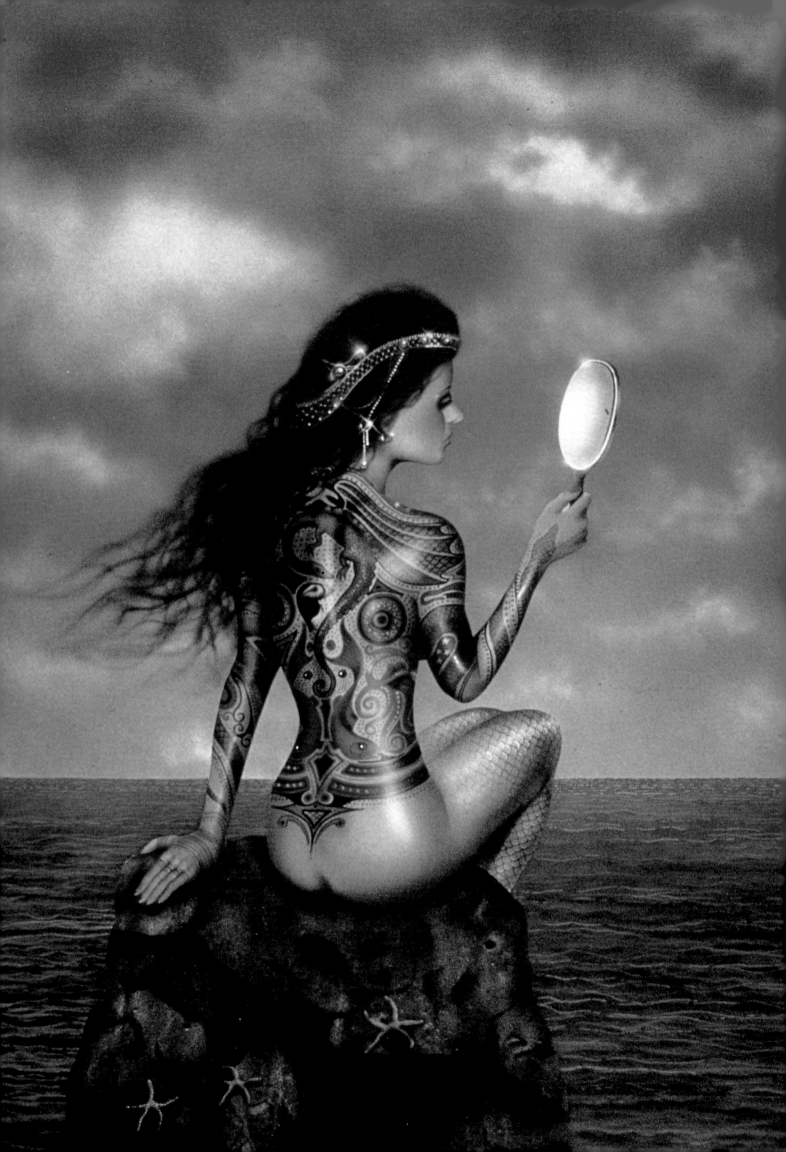

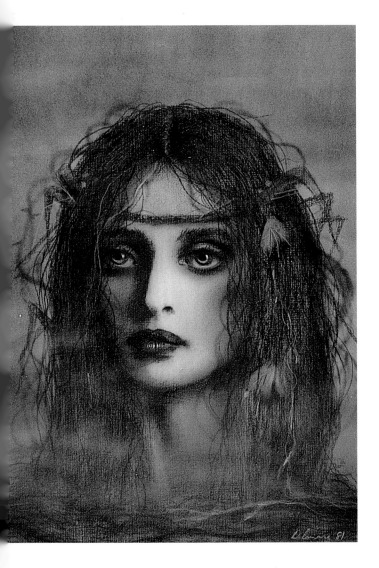

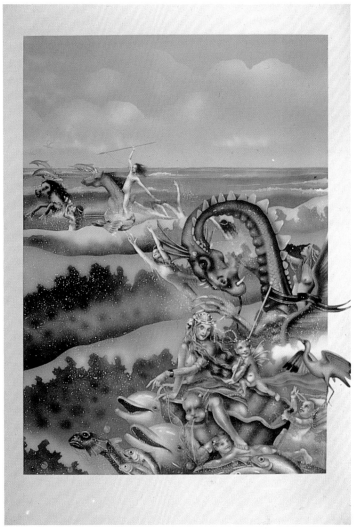

◁ MERMAID'S LOOKING GLASS
1985 Gouache 18 x 27in (45 x 67cm)
Traditionally mermaids are absorbed in their own beauty, but here the mirror is also a symbol or echo of the sea.

△ MERMAID FACE 1981
Gouache 8 x 11in (20 x 27cm)
Despite the stark realism of this face, no model was used; the image rose wholly from Delamare's imagination. The aim was to capture a mermaid's penetrating eyes, and the vaguely menacing result is enhanced by steaming water.

◁ PROCESSION OF NEREIDS 1981
Gouache 16 x 20in (40 x 50cm)
The Nereids are possibly the earliest recorded mermaids, or at least their precursors, since they are not usually depicted as having tails. They are described in classical mythology as being the fifty daughters of the sea-god Nereus and his lovely wife Doris. These sea-nymphs had none of the ambiguity of later mermaids; their exquisite singing voices were employed purely for entertaining their father, and as far as possible they tried to guard sailors against the perils of the deep.

▷ MERMAID 1980
Pencil and ink 8 x 13in (20 x 32cm)
The result of a friend doing a series of poses. Delamare really enjoys drawing as an art form in itself, not merely as a preliminary to painting (for which, in fact, he generally does only very rough thumbnail sketches). The shading is achieved by airbrushing ink over a pencilled outline.

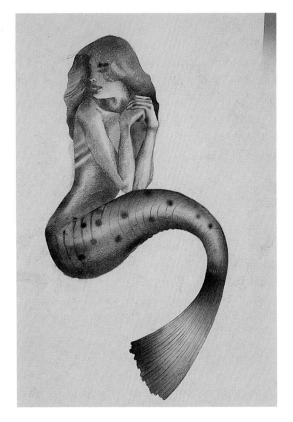

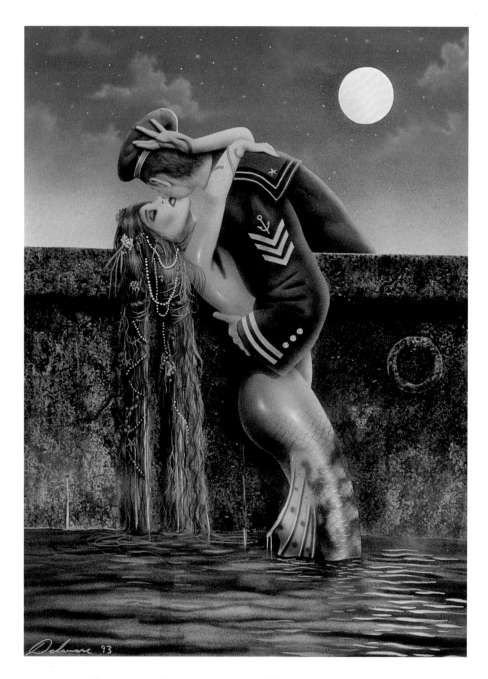

△ **MERMAID AND SAILOR** 1993

Acrylic 20 x 26in (50 x 65cm)

This is a slight reworking of an earlier painting, the original of which was sold and the transparency lost. It captures one of the crucial elements of the mermaid myth – the touching of two different worlds. Hovering in the background is the question of whether or not the sailor will choose the underwater world.

▷ **MERMAID AND CHILD** 1981

Gouache 16 x 20in (40 x 50cm)

An echo of traditional Madonna paintings.

▷ ▷ **MERMAID BIRTH** 1982

Gouache 11 x 20in (27 x 50cm)

The lighting effect here is something Delamare is particularly pleased with. Lighting faces from below usually gives them a sinister cast, but here the result is quite angelic. The mermaid is a rare two-tailed variety.

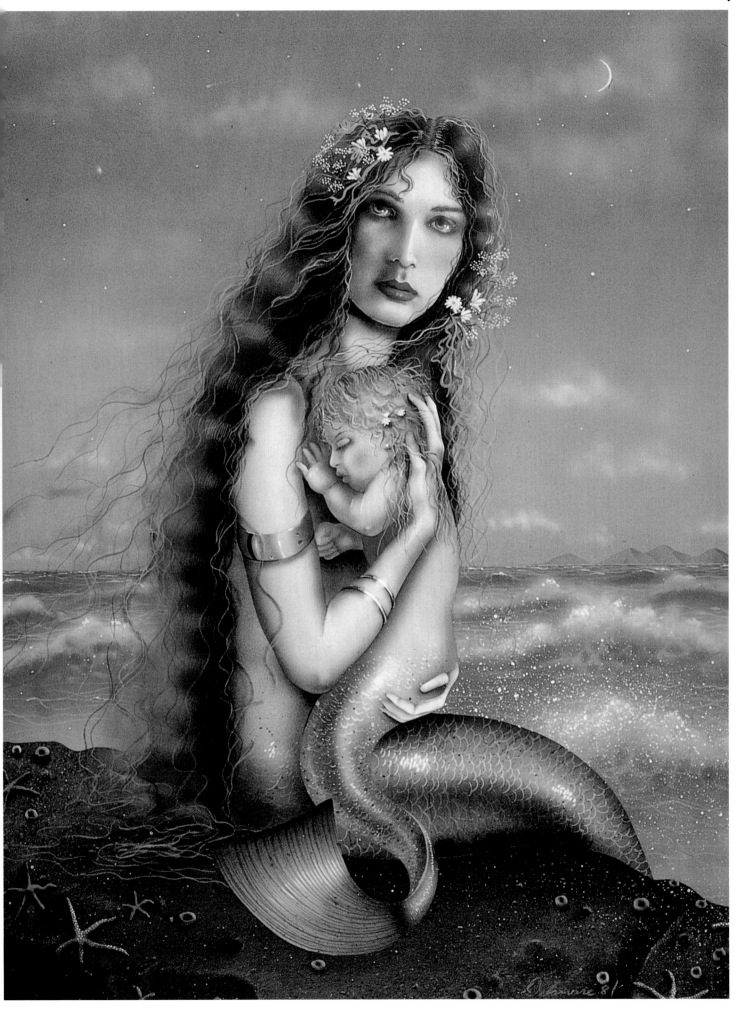

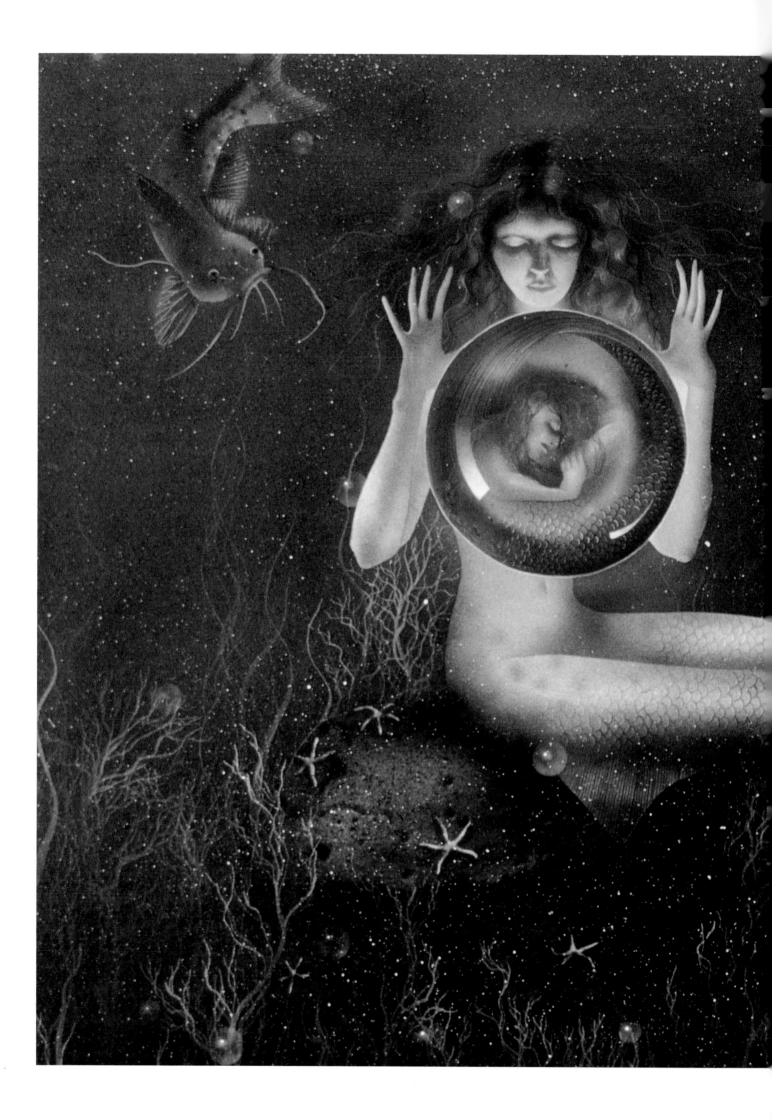

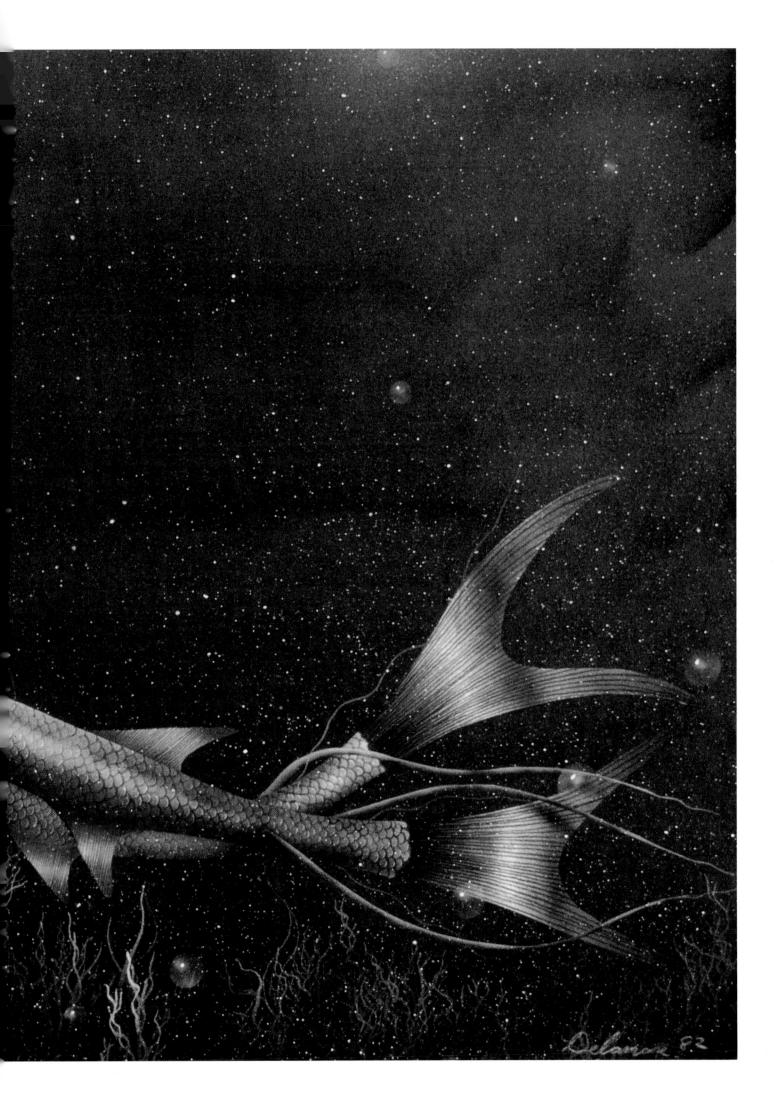

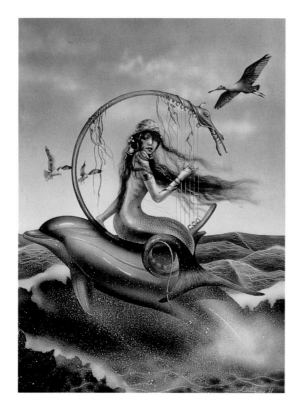

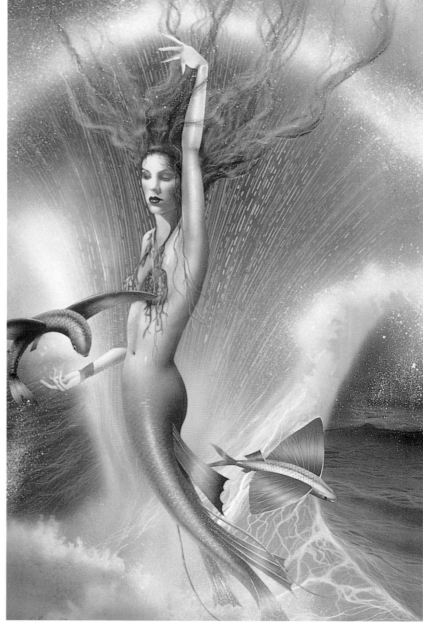

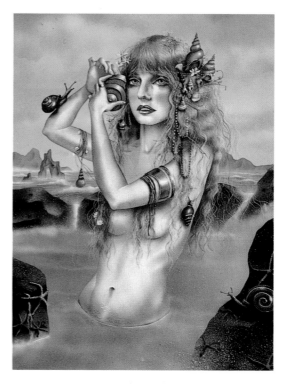

△ **THE HARP OF POSEIDON** 1981
Gouache 16 x 20in (40 x 50cm)

◁ **MERMAID AND FLYING FISH**
1983
Gouache 16 x 20in (40 x 50cm)
For years Delamare thought flying fish
were as much a myth as mermaids, so
he was delighted to stumble on the
truth in an encyclopedia. Suspended
between two worlds, the mermaid
appears to be controlling the waves,
which is one of her reputed powers.

▷
MERMAID WITH SHELLS 1981
Gouache 16 x 20in (40 x 50cm)

▷ ▷ **ON THE DRAGON'S BACK**
1985 *Gouache 18 x 24in (45 x 60cm)*
As his paintings are so often based on
live models, Delamare occasionally
finds himself being pestered for a tele-
phone number by acquaintances who
have fallen in love with one of his
painted ladies. This was particularly
the case with one model, who has a
certain ethereal, unattainable, almost
mermaid-like quality, which cuts
through the defences and sets many
male hearts aquiver. Needless to say,
the artist has kept the number to himself, but in fact, it hardly matters
because the lady is unashamedly gay.

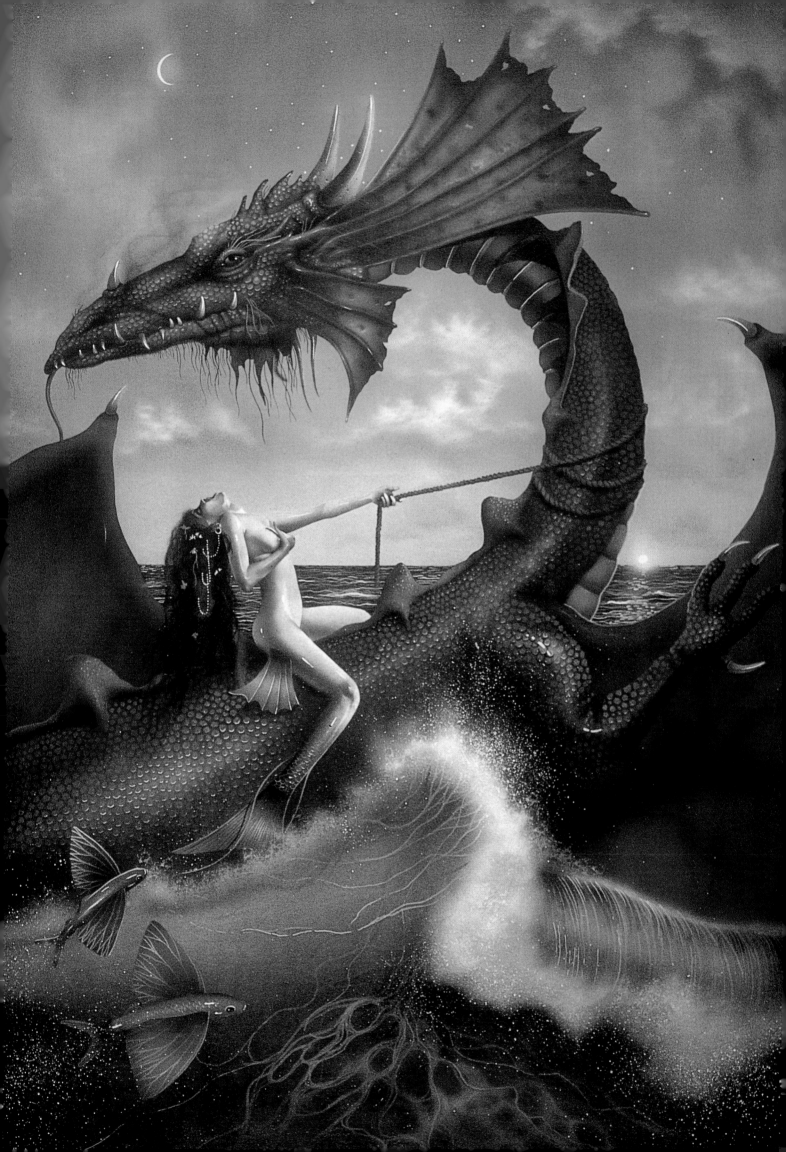

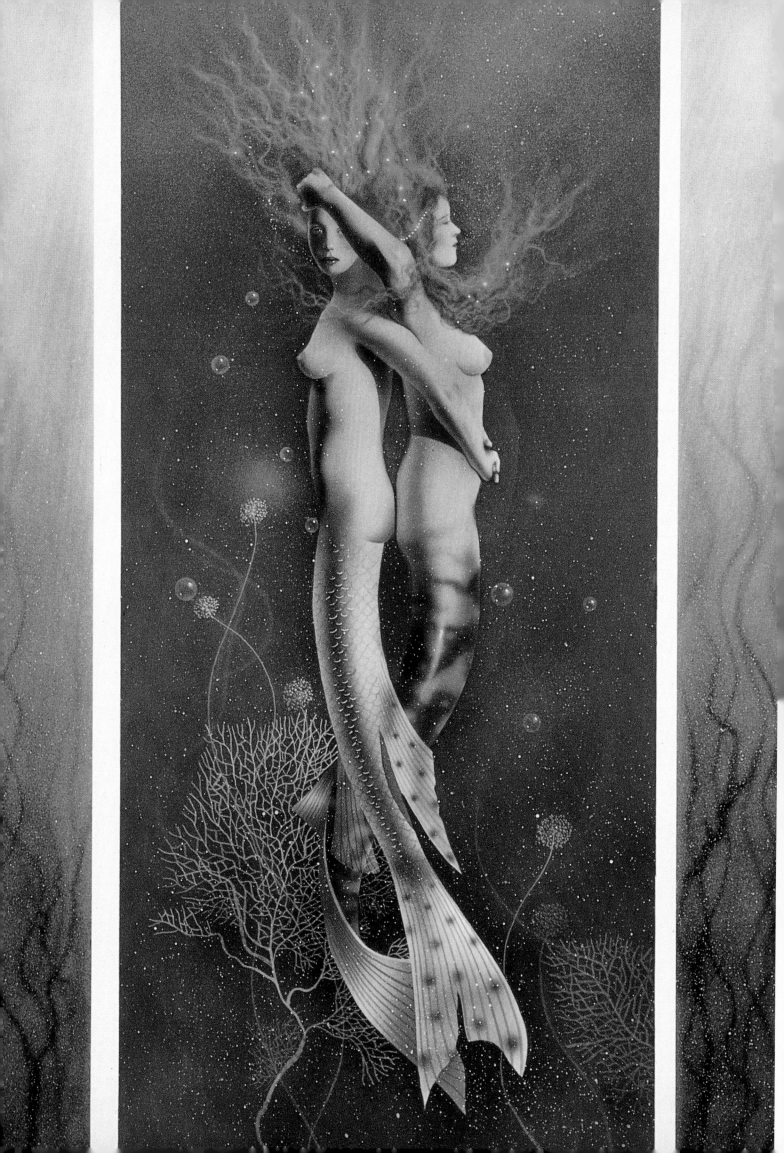

◁ **MARYANNE AND SEASONS** 1993
Acrylic 26 x 32in (65 x 80cm)
This piece resulted from a series of
photographs exploring the idea of an
underwater dance – the ultimate in
gracefulness. For Delamare the apparent weightlessness of mermaids in
their natural environment is one of their
main attractions as a subject: it gives
him a tremendous freedom in which to
compose his pictures. Another area of
artistic freedom comes from the wonderful design possibilities of their tails.

▷ **GUARDIAN OF THE NEREID** 1985
Gouache 18 x 26in (45 x 65cm)
Following descriptions by writers such
as Pliny in the first century AD, this
nymph is shown with a tail.

In Europe, until about the eighteenth century, mermaids were widely believed to be real, and accounts of sightings were taken seriously. Authorities such as Pliny and Pausanias in the first centuries of the Christian era wrote as if they had first-hand knowledge of the creatures and thus gave them respectability. There was a growing flood of recorded sightings and encounters, building to a peak in the Middle Ages when historians and travel writers passed on the tales they had heard without pausing to question their plausibility. The waters round the British Isles were believed to be especially populous, but authoritative tales of encounters with mermaids came also from Holland, Poland and France, backed by a wealth of folklore from everywhere else connected with the sea.

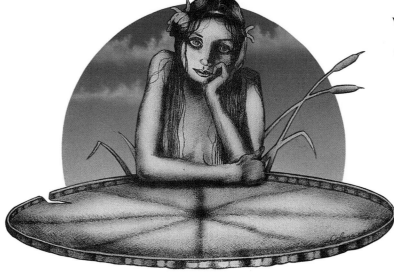

MERMAID RESTING ON LILY PAD 1981
Pencil and gouache
10 x 12in (25 x 30cm)

From France came the legend of Melusina, a beauty who captured the heart of Raymond, Count of Poitiers. She married him on condition that she could spend one day a week in complete privacy. All was fine till one day Raymond's curiosity got the better of him. Spying through the keyhole on her having a bath, he discovered that he had married a mermaid who was 'from the navel downwards in likeness of a great serpent, the tail as great and thick as a barrel, and so long was it she made it to touch oftimes, while Raymond beheld her, the roof of the chamber that was right high.'

When he confronted her with his discovery, she vanished. To commemorate the event Raymond incorporated a mermaid into the family coat of arms, the House of Lusignan. This example was soon followed by other European families, such as the Houses of Luxembourg, Rohan and Sassanaye. Suddenly, they all discovered that they too had a mermaid somewhere in their ancestry.

With the great maritime expeditions of the sixteenth and seventeenth centuries fresh sightings were reported from as far afield as the Americas and the Far East. Many of these were dismissed at the time as sailors' yarns but some, as with UFO and Loch Ness monster sightings these days, came from apparently sober-minded, conservative individuals with no axe to grind.

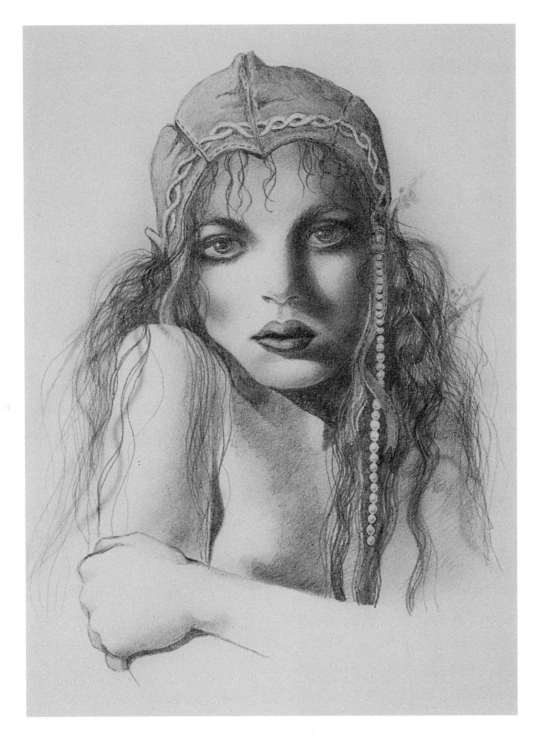

MERMAID WITH MAGIC CAP 1990
Pencil and ink 12 x 12in (30 x 30cm)

▷ ▷ **THE GATES OF ATLANTIS**
1981
Gouache 12 x 18in (30 x 45cm)

The chance was taken here to explore the diffused lighting and monochromatic tendency of underwater scenes. Most of the painting was simply an exercise in imagination, with photographic references being used to sharpen up some details.

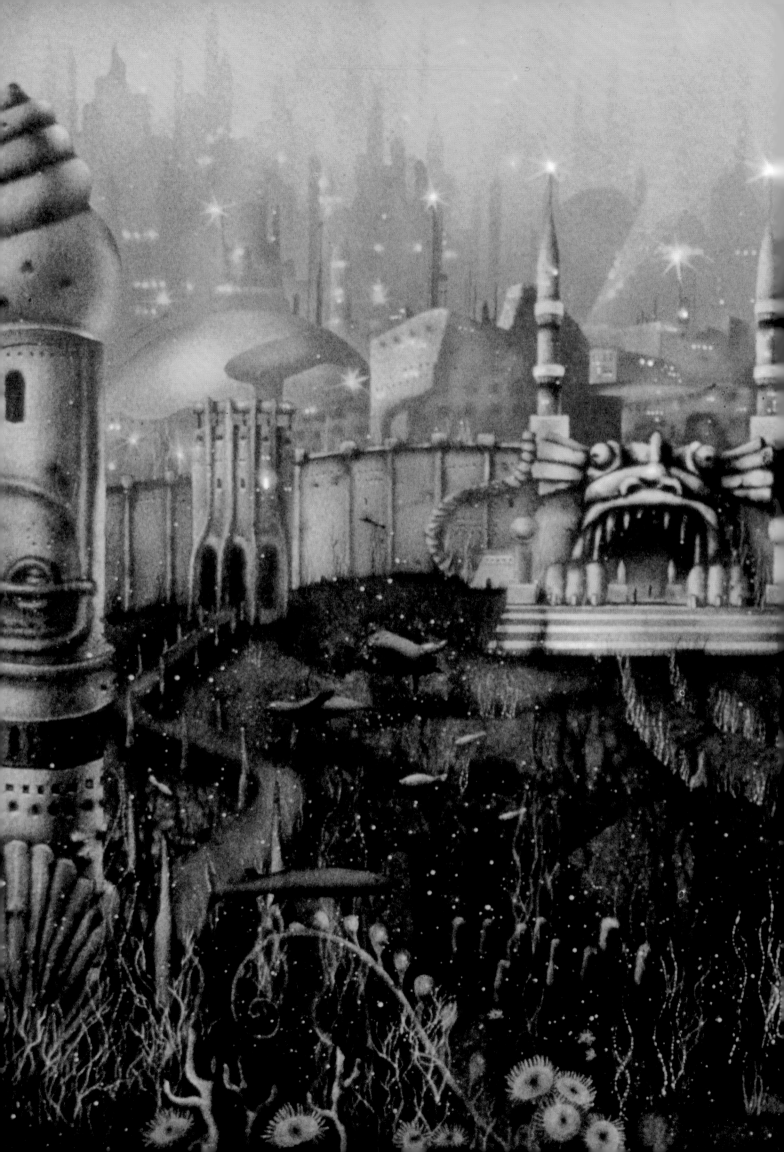

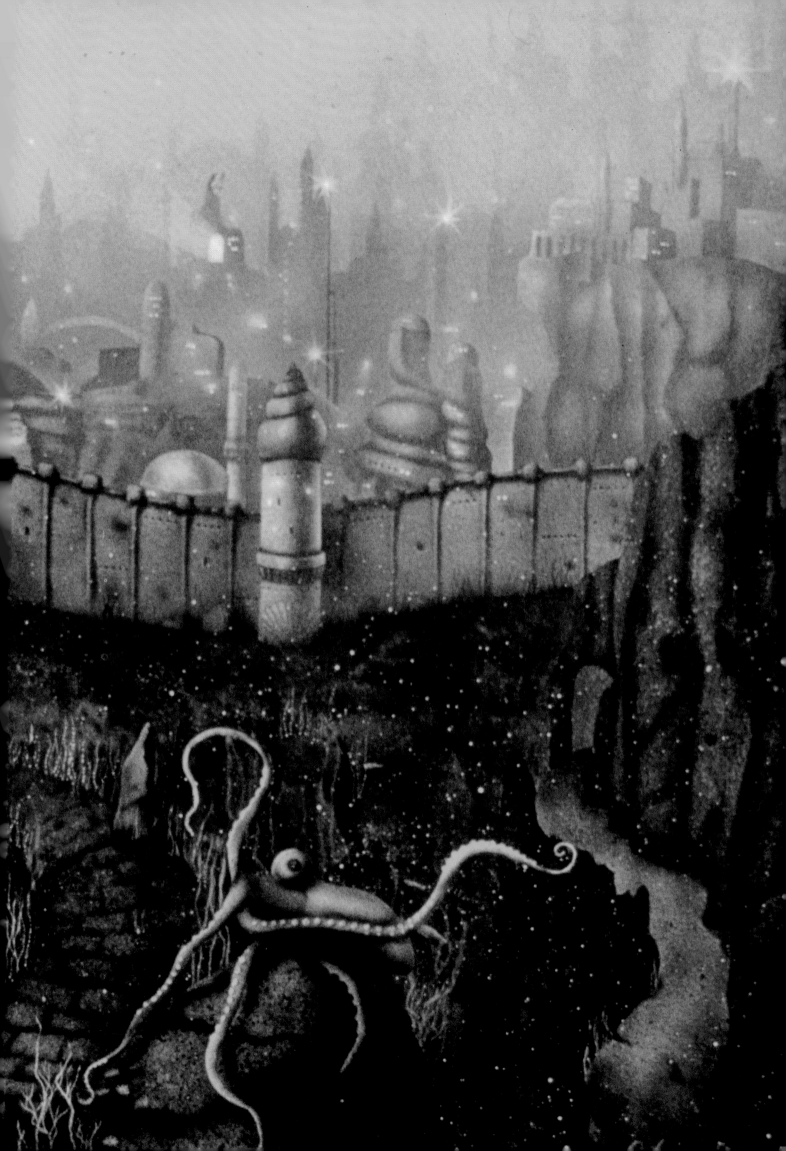

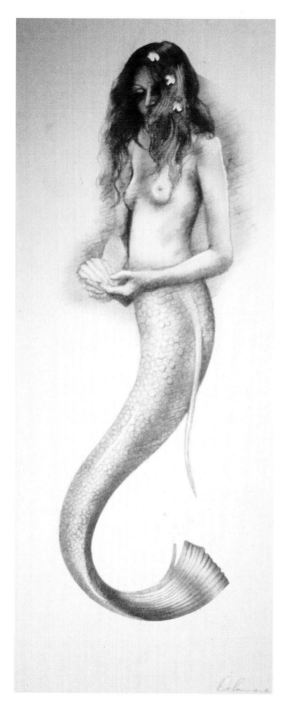

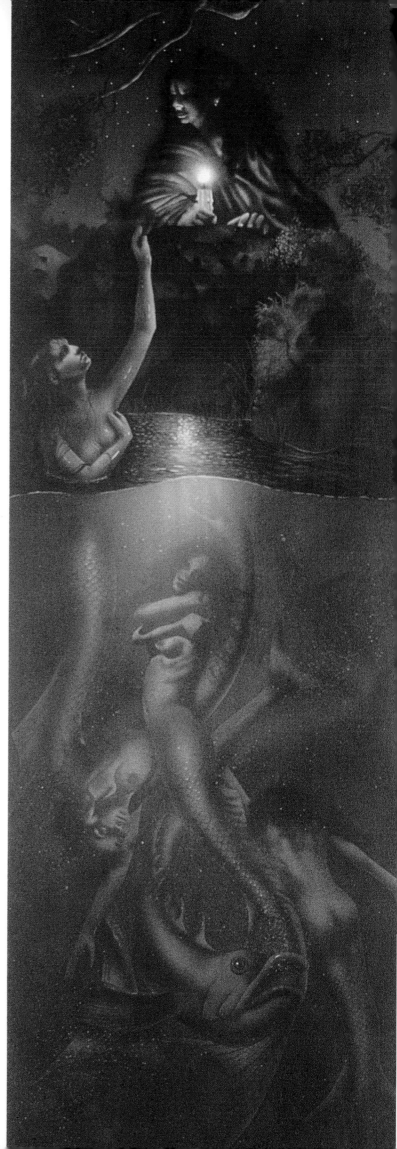

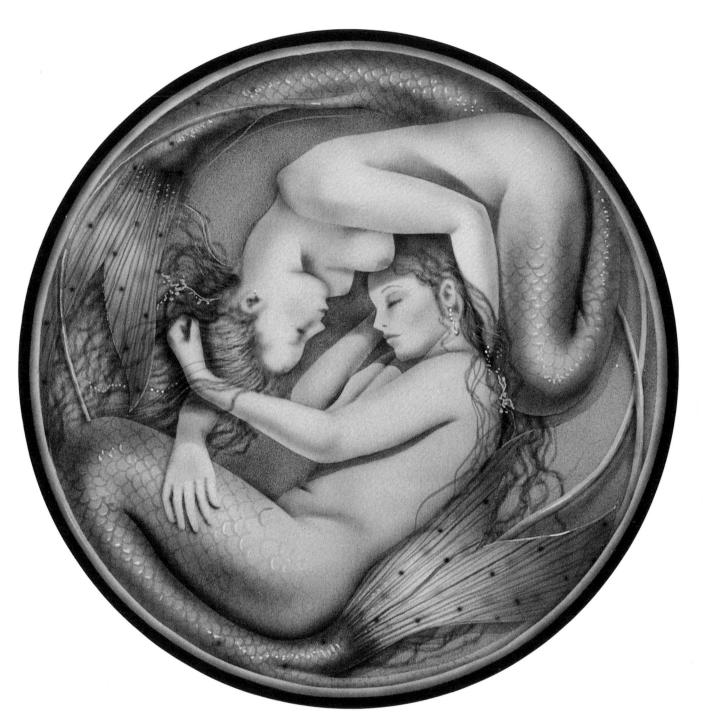

◁ ◁ **MERMAID OPENING SHELL**
1982
Pencil 5 x 7in (12 x 17cm)

◁ **MERMAID POOL** 1981
Gouache 9 x 20in (22 x 50cm)
The theme here is the interesting inter-action between two worlds. The pic-ture portrays the mutual fascination on both sides and the weighing up of

what crossing the divide will cost. In keeping with the symbolism, the rather formal composition at the top becomes increasingly chaotic towards the bottom.

△ **SLEEPING MERMAIDS** 1993
Acrylic 12in (30cm) diameter
This portrays an almost Celtic Yin-Yang symbol.

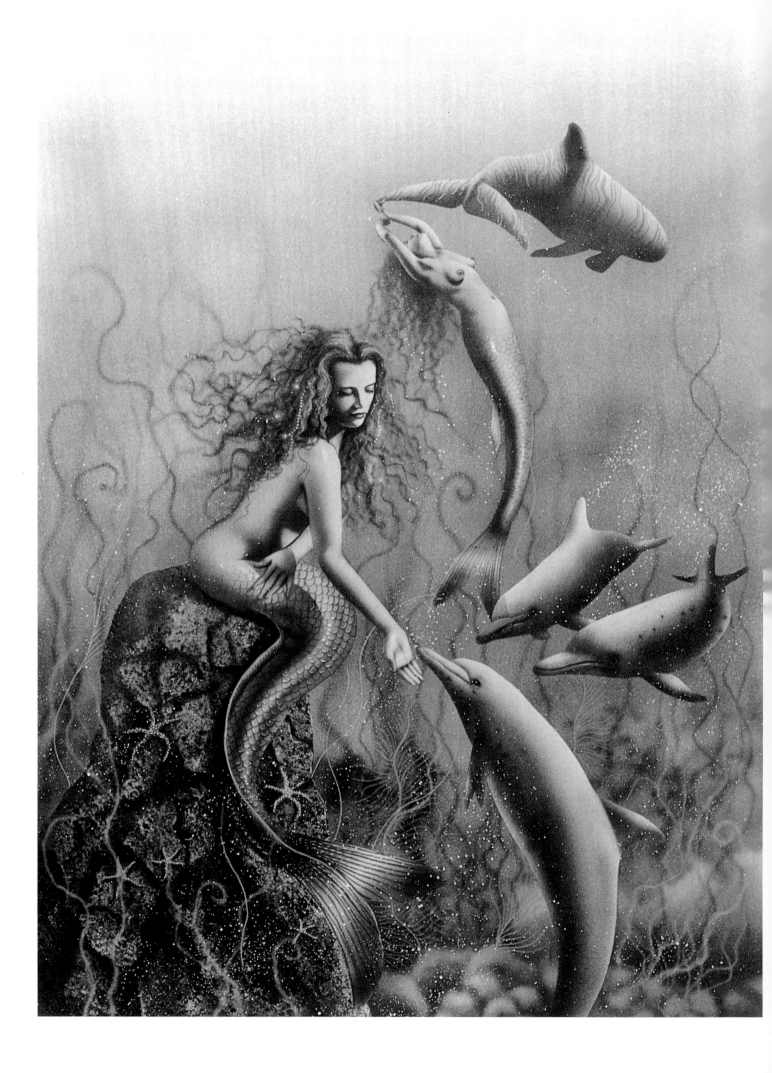

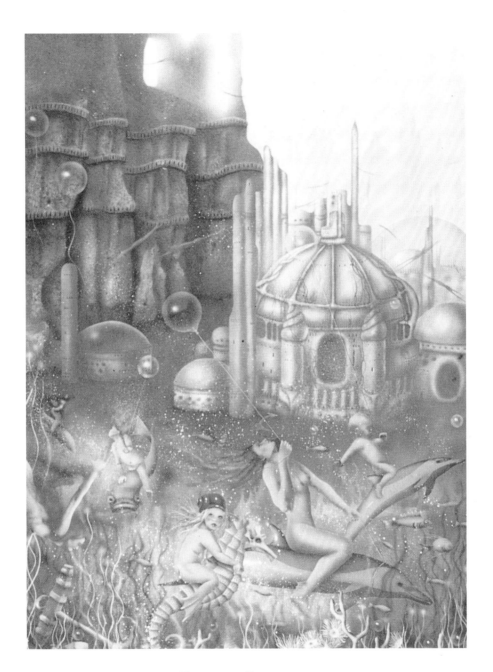

◁ **FEEDING THE DOLPHINS** 1993
Acrylic 14 x 20in (35 x 50cm)

△ **UNDERWATER CITY** 1981
Gouache 16 x 20in (40 x 50cm)
An idealistic vision of underwater life
based on the assumption that all the
creatures there would live in symbiotic
harmony.

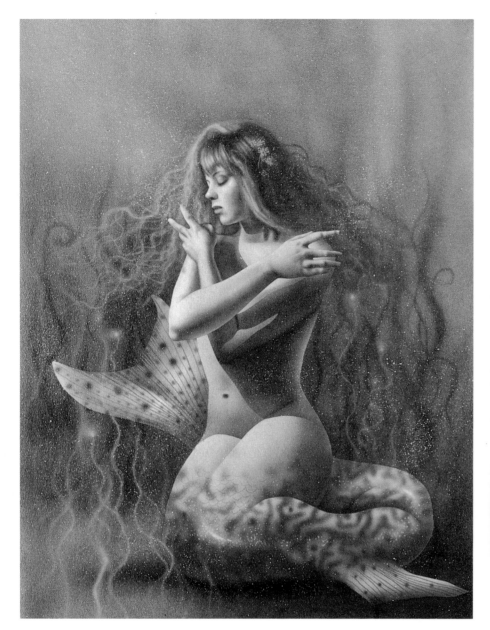

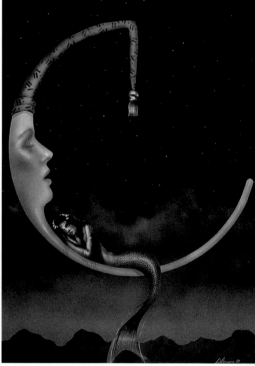

△ **MARYANNE** 1993

Acrylic 14 x 20in (35 x 50cm)

Shortly before doing this picture
Delamare was commissioned to illustrate Cinderella (of which more will be
said later). During the project the problem arose of casting models for the
wicked and, of course, very ugly step-
sisters. A diplomatic alternative to
mortally offending any female friends
or neighbours was suggested – dress
up a couple of men. This was done
and the ensuing sketches sent off for

approval. They were returned with
much praise from the publishers,
except for one problem: the ugly step-
sisters looked like a couple of trans-
vestites and could something be done
to improve them?

Eventually it was decided that
Delamare's girlfriend, Maryanne, would
model for the sisters and just pull ugly
faces. The end result pleased every-
one, and by way of recompense
Delamare painted this portrait of her
transformed into a mermaid.

◁ **MERMAID AND THE MOON** 1985

Gouache 18 x 24in (45 x 60cm)

▷ **BATHING IN MOONLIGHT** 1993

Acrylic 14 x 20in (35 x 50cm)

Delamare experimented here with the
texture of the tail, giving it a spiky,
almost armoured appearance, which
contrasts strongly with the soft flesh.

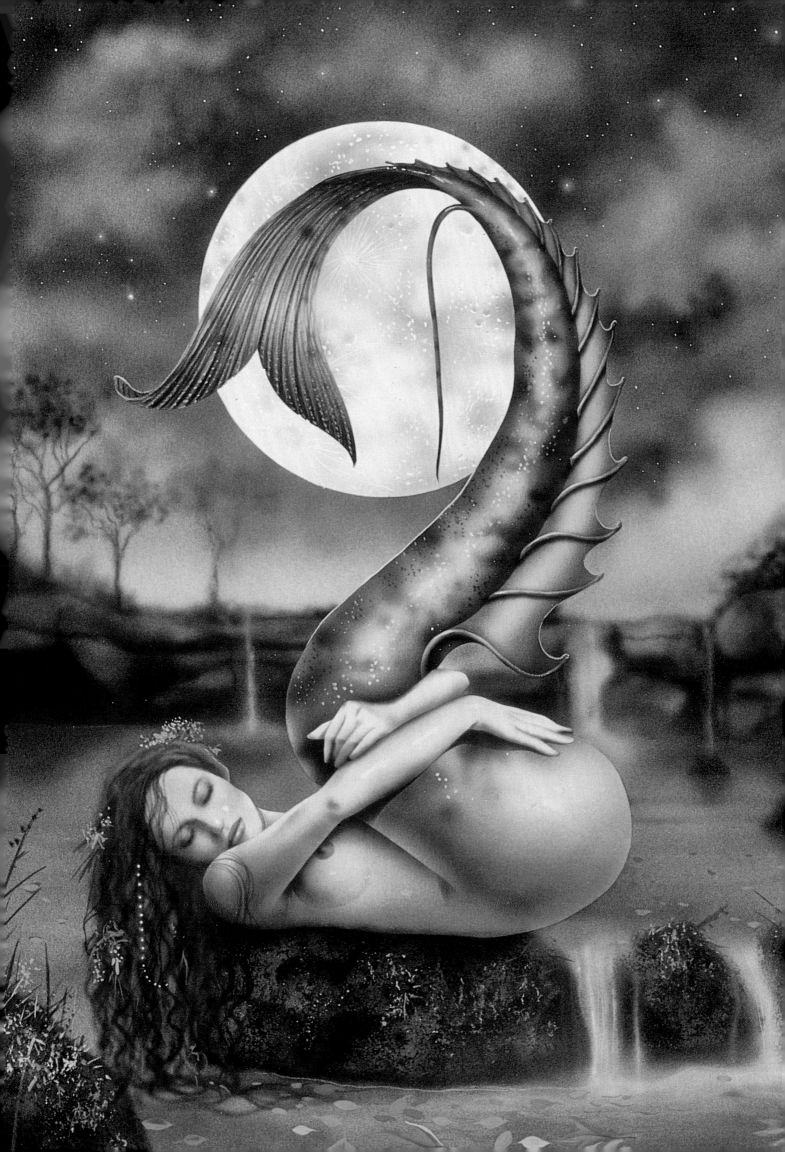

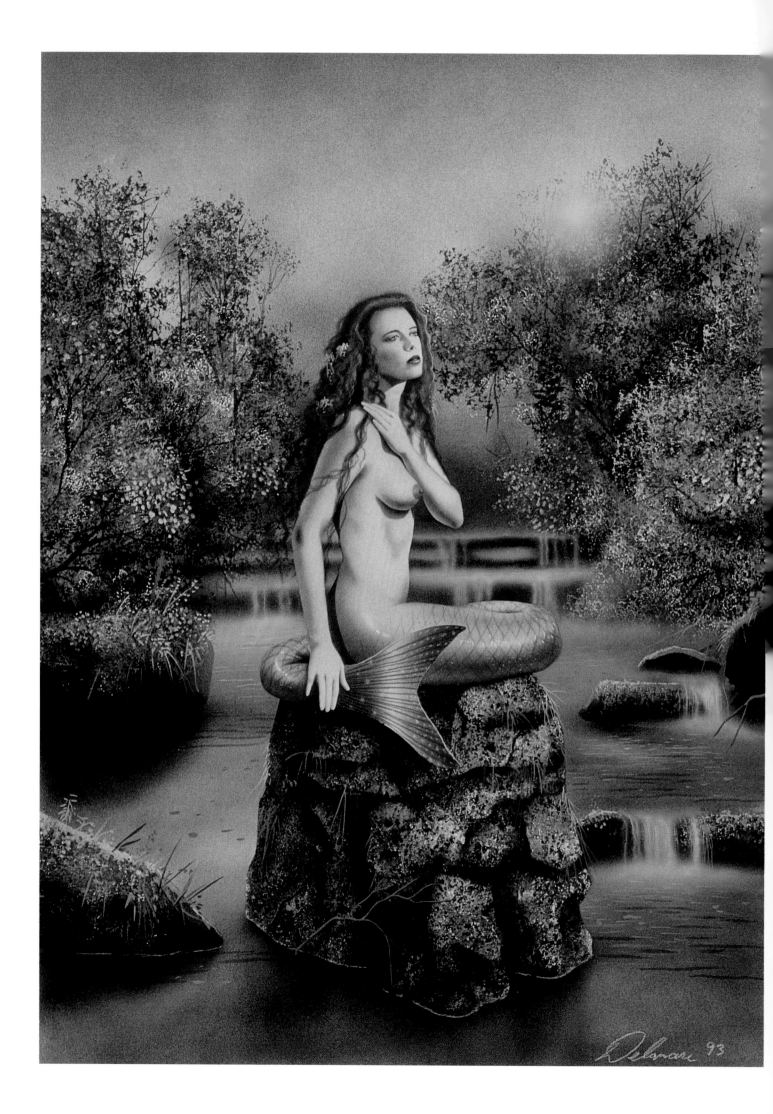

Delmare 93

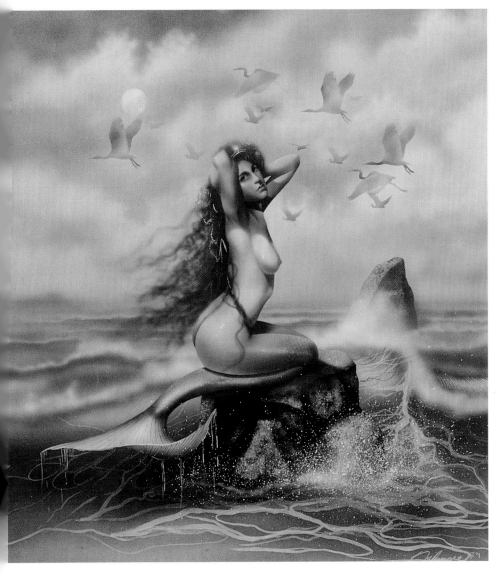

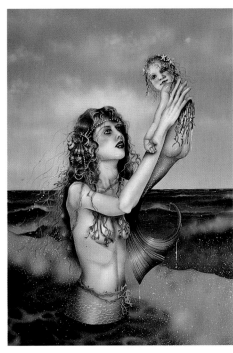

◁ **UNDINE** 1993

Acrylic 14 x 20in (35 x 50cm)

Paracelsus, the sixteenth-century philosopher and alchemist, subscribed to the view that 'undines', or water nymphs, possessed all human qualities except an immortal soul. They could, however, acquire this through marriage with a mortal. In time, his views inspired Hans Christian Andersen's fable *The Little Mermaid*, and the popular nineteenth-century romance *Undine* by de la Motte Fouque, whose theme was the tragic consequences that are usually attendant on such marriages.

△ **DONNA** 1989

Acrylic 17 x 19in (43 x 48cm)

The model used in this picture later went on to work in a waterbed store.

◁ **A GIFT FROM THE SEA** 1981

Gouache 16 x 20in (40 x 50cm)

SIRENS

Sirens are the downside of mermaids, with the complication that it is often impossible to tell the difference until too late. Both have shape-shifting abilities, and both attract men by their beauty and irresistible singing. The difference is their character and intention.

The reason such myths survive is that, on the same level as dreams, they address perennial human problems and situations. With sirens it is that of being attracted to something inherently perilous yet irresistible. Their male counterparts are, I suppose, wolves or, perhaps more closely, vampires.

We all know people who have entered a relationship knowing full well that it will lead to emotional disaster, yet have pressed on none the less. They may post mental buoys in advance marking where self-preservation indicates they should get out, but once the siren voices start singing such wisdom seems petty. All too soon the pit, which was foreseen at the outset, is tumbled into.

The earliest accounts of sirens describe them as Greek river deities who, apart from an excessive pride in their voices, had no great faults. But they fell foul, first of Aphrodite, who punished them for being rebellious to love by giving them the bodies of birds, and second of the Muses, whom they challenged to a musical contest but lost. The vanquishing Muses pulled out the sirens' feathers, forcing them to hide among the rocks off the southern coast of Italy. Here, legend has it, Odysseus outwitted them by having his crew plug their ears with wax and having himself strapped to the mast so he could hear the sirens' uncanny song without being able to respond. This scene has been a favourite with artists down the ages.

The sirens' appearance has changed with time. On ancient Greek vases they appear, as Homer described them, with bird-like bodies and human heads. Gradually, they have taken on a more mermaid-like body, reflecting the changing popular conception of sirens.

With the eighteenth century and the Age of Reason, scepticism began to encroach on the myth, but not without a few setbacks. For example, the Danish Royal Commission sent an expedition to the Faroe Islands in 1723 to examine and test the truth of the phenomenon. The expedition report claimed that a black-bearded merman with deep-set eyes happened to pop up beside the boat to answer a few questions. This proof was not enough though, and in the late eighteenth and nineteenth centuries people wanted more concrete evidence. The response was a rash of exhibitions of stuffed mermaids, including one staged by circus owner P.T. Barnum. All the exhibits, however, were soon proved to be fakes. They were a far cry from the glamorous temptresses of legend, being as grotesque as they were contrived.

All of this did little to suppress interest in mermaids as figures of the imagination. Indeed, the nineteenth century saw an upsurge in their popularity, as demonstrated by the Pre-Raphaelites and Symbolists in art, and in literature by writers as diverse as Hans Christian Andersen and Oscar Wilde. The twentieth century has seen continuing fascination on many levels from light entertainment to high art, and as Delamare's paintings show, the vein is far from exhausted.

Mermaids are one of those perennial themes that each age interprets in its own way. The alchemists probably hit the nail on the head long ago when they interpreted the mermaid visions that arose in the course of their investigations as images of the unconscious soul. As such there is no limit to the number of ways in which they can be interpreted: it all depends on the observer and the climate of the times in which he or she is living. On the other hand, perhaps this simply reflects the fact that after their failure with Odysseus, and later Orpheus, the sirens decided that their cover was blown and that disguising themselves as their more popular cousins, the Nereids, would restore their popularity.

SIREN IN CIRCLE 1982
Gouache 14in (35cm) diameter

Delamare often feels that the peculiarity of objects under water is a large part of the appeal of these pictures – the mysterious way that light is diffused and the way objects melt into the background as in a fog. The colours also tend towards being monochromatic in the background, thus accentuating the foreground figures and making for strong compositions.

The dark mood of these siren pictures is fairly untypical of Delamare's work as a whole. They demonstrate that it is perhaps by choice and temperament that most of his pictures are so remarkably cheerful and uplifting. For a rounded view of the subject of mermaids it is necessary to consider their dark side, and he has shown himself perfectly capable of this, but the dark side of life generally seems much less of a preoccupation to Delamare than its wonder and mysteriousness.

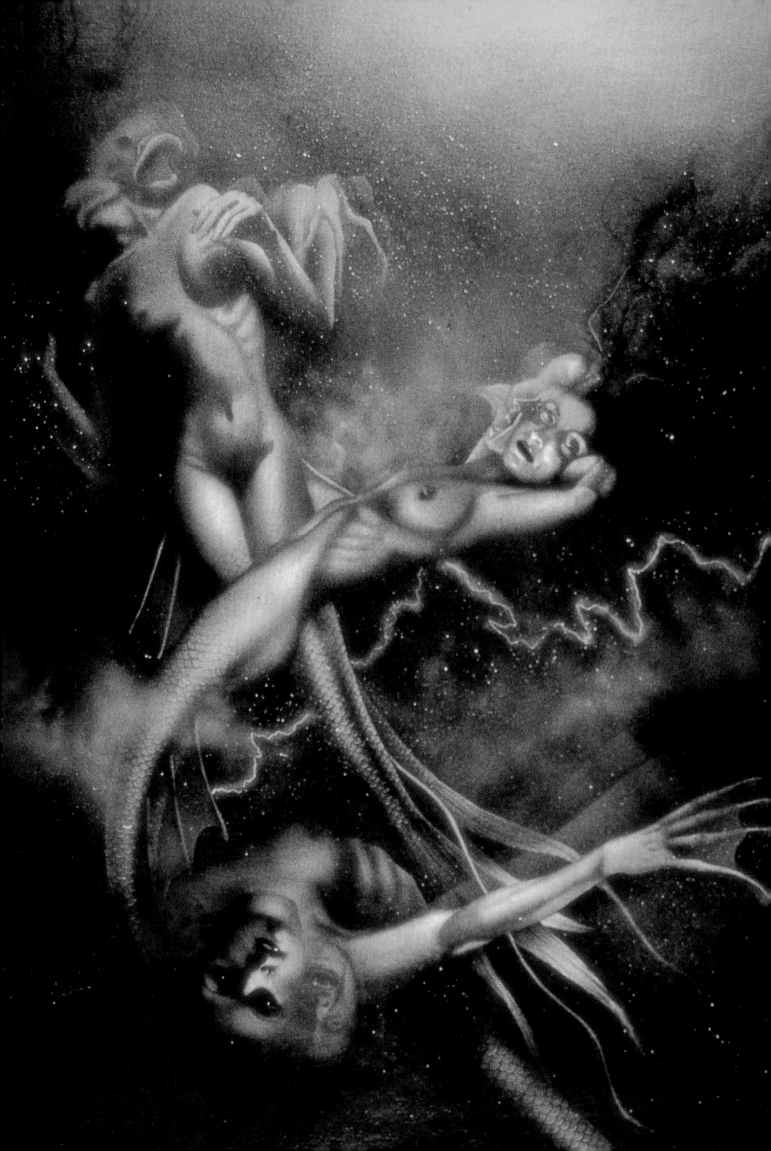

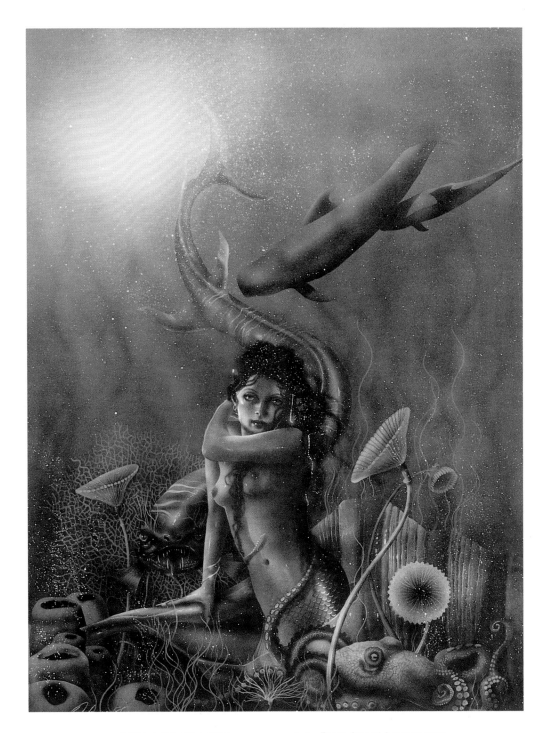

◁ **SHAPE SHIFTING** 1982

Gouache 16 x 20in (40 x 50cm)

A creepy conglomeration of all the elements historically associated with sirens.

△ **FULL FATHOM FIVE** 1986

Gouache 18 x 24in (45 x 60cm)

▷▷ **DAVY JONES' LOCKER** 1982

Gouache 16 x 20in (40 x 50cm)

Believe it or not, says Delamare, the victim is submitting freely.

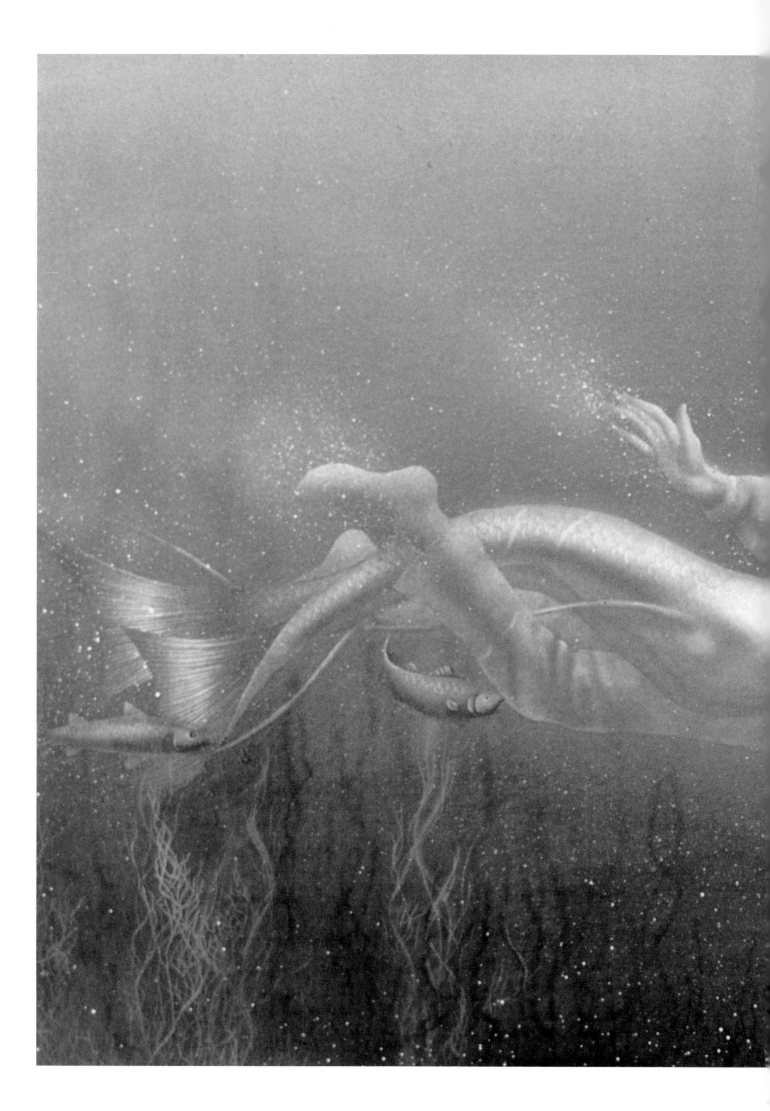

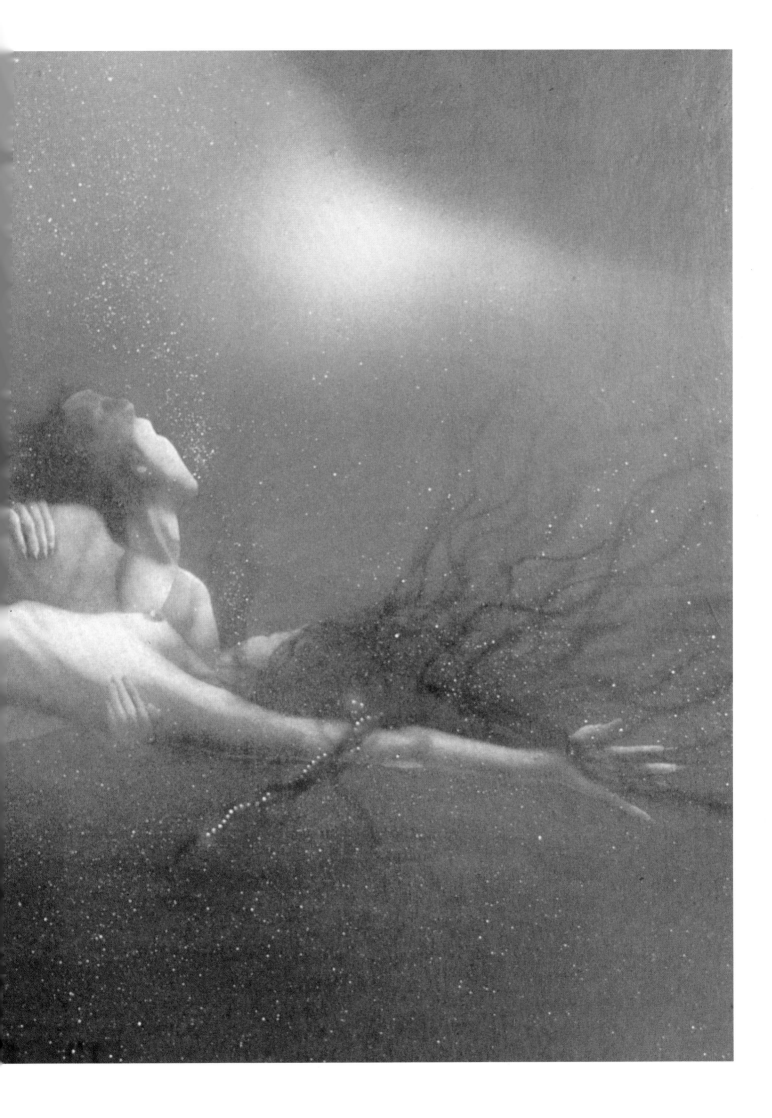

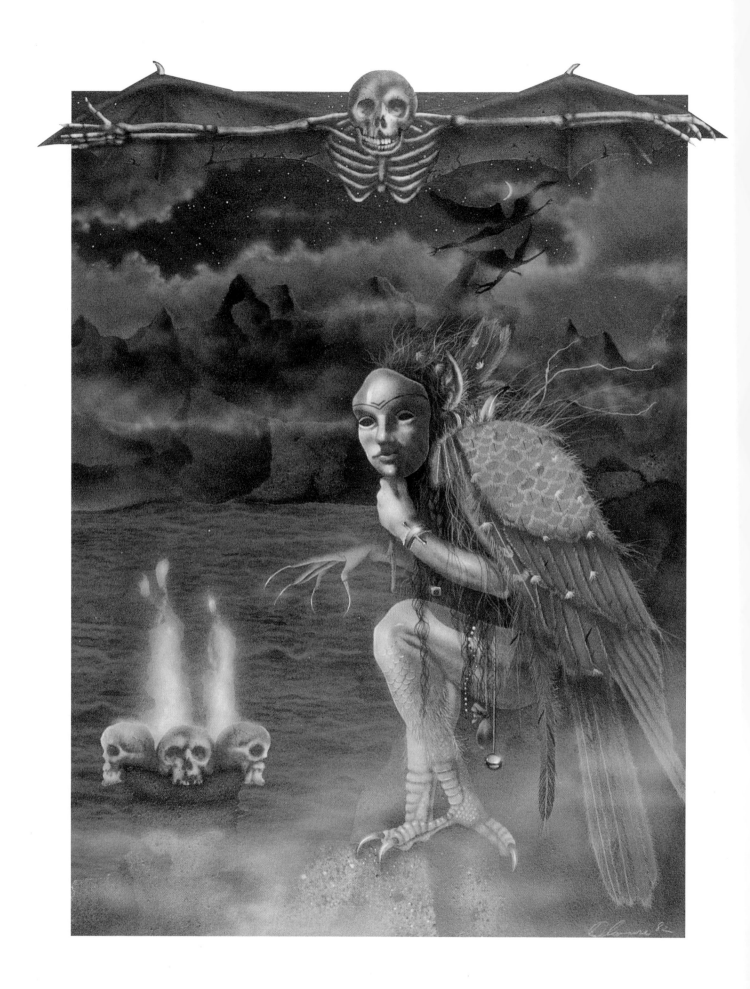

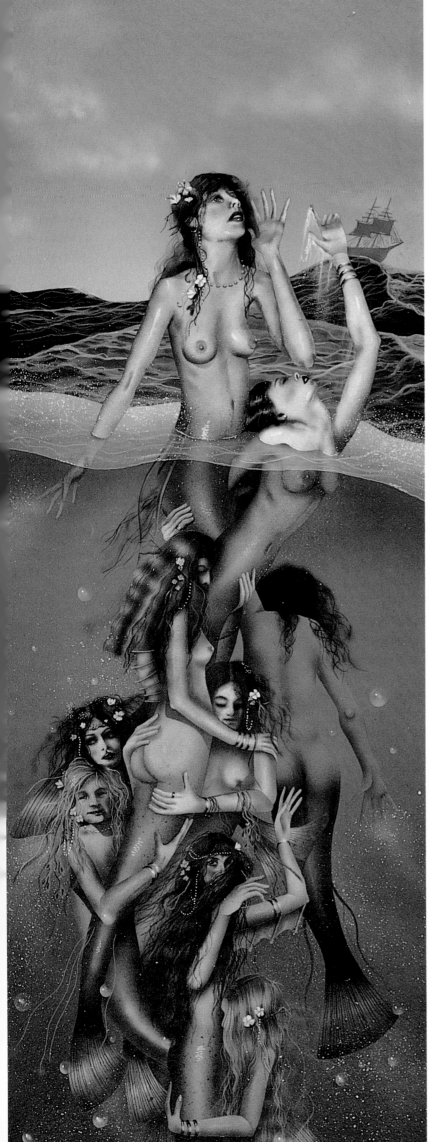

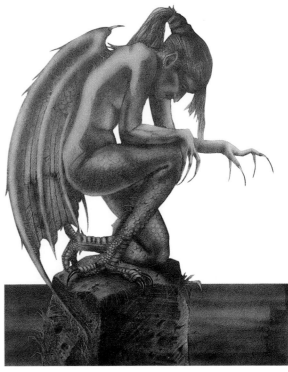

△ **SIREN** 1983

Pencil and ink 9 x 12in (22 x 30cm)

Delamare has found that a test of a
model's friendship is whether or not
they mind you depicting them in an
unflattering way.

◁ ◁ **SIREN WITH MASK** 1983

Gouache 16 x 20in (40 x 50 cm)

The idea behind this depiction of an
early siren was to capture the point
that the siren's beauty is always a
mask of some sort.

◁ **THE CALL OF THE SIRENS** 1982

Gouache 10 x 20in (25 x 50cm)

A traditional treatment of the subject of
sirens, with them beckoning ships
using a tip-of-the-iceberg effect. The
languid temptress at the top is
supported by a frenetic column of
other sirens.

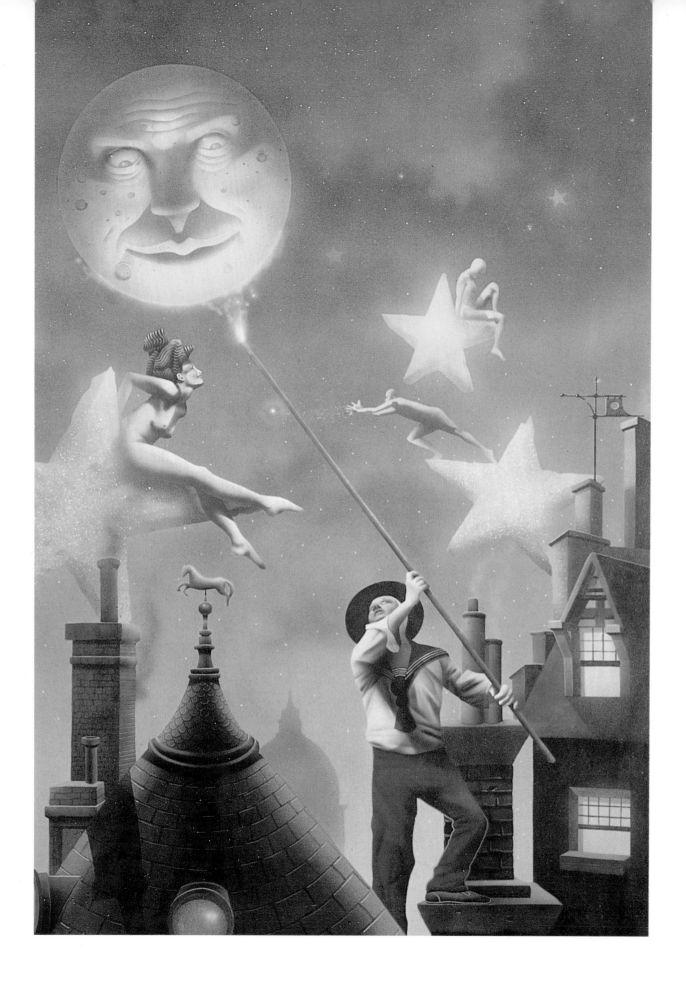

EAST OF THE MOON

One consequence of being an only child is that Delamare soon learned to be resourceful in entertaining himself. From an early age he used to stage 'creative adventures' and loved drawing, painting and making books. His mother loved books, so he read avidly from childhood, early favourites being *The Wind in the Willows* and the *Rupert* stories (not available in the USA, but shipped over by English relations).

Although he loved art, he was not considered outstanding at school; creative certainly, but not to the extent that he was deemed worthy of special tuition. Looking back on this he thinks he may just have been shy of doing art formally, sensing even then that it is a subject which cannot be taught, only assimilated.

Was he later prompted towards becoming an artist by his family? Not directly, he says, though they were supportive. There are no painters that he knows of among his family and forebears, 'but there is a generalized artistic family background which is manifested in entertainment'. His English grandmother was a performer in British vaudeville, specializing for a while in a dance called Legmania. She was a vivid and original character whom Delamare feels may well have influenced him in wanting to do something unconventional with his life. Her father was a tenor who moved to Boston in search of a new life. When he was established, he sent for his wife to join him but she refused to live in 'cowboy country'. Thus the family's divided loyalties between the US and Britain were established well before David came on the scene.

The theatrical background explains much of Delamare's approach to work and also his frustrated, but not serious, desire to be a theatre director. That ambition was quenched by an eighteen-month stint as a professional musician, which taught him that he was not naturally

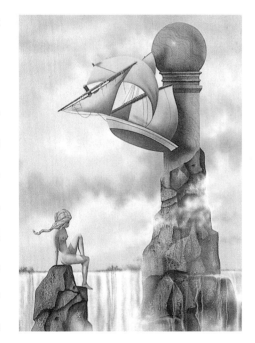

IDYLL 1987

Gouache 18 x 24in (45 x 57cm)

This reflects Delamare's ongoing fascination with things that defy gravity. In fact, in everyday life he is afraid of heights. Aeroplanes do not bother him particularly, but looking over the edge of a tall building or cliff usually induces a serious attack of vertigo. He is very fond of flying dreams though, but for many years these were only possible if he was holding on to his pillow.

suited to working with other artists. At times the friction was exciting, but for him it was 'fire without illumination'. He remains an avid theatre-goer, but his own magic theatre seems set to remain one of the mind, which manifests itself in his paintings, many of which are like theatrical tableaux or scenes from mysterious, marvel-filled plays. He casts the models for his pictures as a director would and sets up his studio very much like a stage for shooting preparatory photographs.

JUST ABOVE THE MAGICAL SEA 1981
Gouache 16 x 20in (40 x 50cm)
The subtitle for this picture could be 'Speculation'. For Delamare the sea is a great metaphor for the unknown – the surface can be seen, but not what lies below...

Finally, he sells his pictures through galleries because that is the way the world works, but what he would really like to do is load them into a wagon and go on a travelling art show, stopping here and there when the mood takes him and setting up an exhibition of pictures for sale.

As an artist, most of Delamare's influences have been oblique. When he first came upon the work of the Surrealists it was not so much a revelation as a relief to find that other people viewed the world in a similar way. His own brand of surrealism developed simply from close observation of the world around him – it always seemed a pretty bizarre place. Most children share this view of course, that is, before they take on the adult illusion that we live in a well-ordered universe. In Delamare's case it was reinforced by circumstances that still, in retrospect, seem quite surreal. For example, as a child he observed the mental decline of some elderly neighbours. After the husband died the wife became a somnambulist and one winter night wandered out into the back garden and was found frozen in some bramble bushes the following morning.

On a lighter, but no less strange, note were the journeys the family used to make every couple of years to visit Delamare's father, who had left the family to become a professional gambler in Nevada – a domestic arrangement which, in itself, seemed quite normal at the time. While driving across the apparently limitless desert, there would occasionally rise out of the distance a gas station planted alone in the middle of nowhere, or a shack by the roadside with a forlorn notice outside trying to tempt travellers to stop a moment and view some marvel such as a two-headed rattlesnake for 25 cents. How such eccentrics survived remains a lingering mystery and a reminder that the world is full of eccentricity for those who know where, or how, to look.

Delamare's pictures have a 'narrative' quality, which is perhaps why his style lends itself so well to book illustration. When working on an individual piece,
though, the narrative usually develops alongside
the imagery. Most pictures spring from an ele-
mental spark which can come from almost
anywhere. For example, while sitting at a bus-
stop a woman with shopping vaguely catches
his eye, then a cat comes strolling along the
wall behind and something clicks. Although he
does not know where it will lead, he knows he has
the core of a new piece.

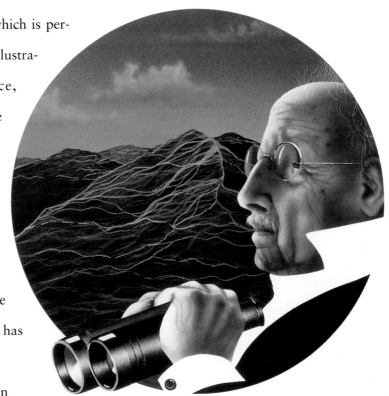

Delamare's initial thoughts when developing an
idea are 'extremely unfocused or abstract. I follow intuition or feeling,
not calculated thought.' He can describe the process of creation only

SEARCHING THE SEAS 1983
Gouache 14 x 14in (35 x 35cm)

by analogy with an old East Indian man he knew who produced wonderful carvings. When asked once:
'How do you do this?', the old man replied that when, say, carving an elephant he merely started with a
block of wood and removed all the parts that did not feel like elephant.

Although he has a considerable grasp of painting technique, it interests Delamare less than composition. He loves working with models, props and lighting, and will often set up a photo session without
any idea of what he is looking for. Then he starts shifting things around until something happens, until
some 'point of departure' presents itself. Sometimes nothing happens, but it is rare.

He almost always listens to music when working – usually jazz, classical string quartets or chamber
music. Delamare feels it is important to have a slight distraction to 'unfocus' the creative process. Too
much concentration can be crippling, as Goethe found in the eighteenth century. In the absence of a
private orchestra or a stereo, Goethe used to keep a pile of rotting fruit beside his work desk.

Thinking too much about where your ideas come from can be frightening, says Delamare: 'It can
quickly lead to paranoia, because if you don't know where your ideas come from, one day they may just
stop. The ephemeral quality of creation makes for anxiety.'

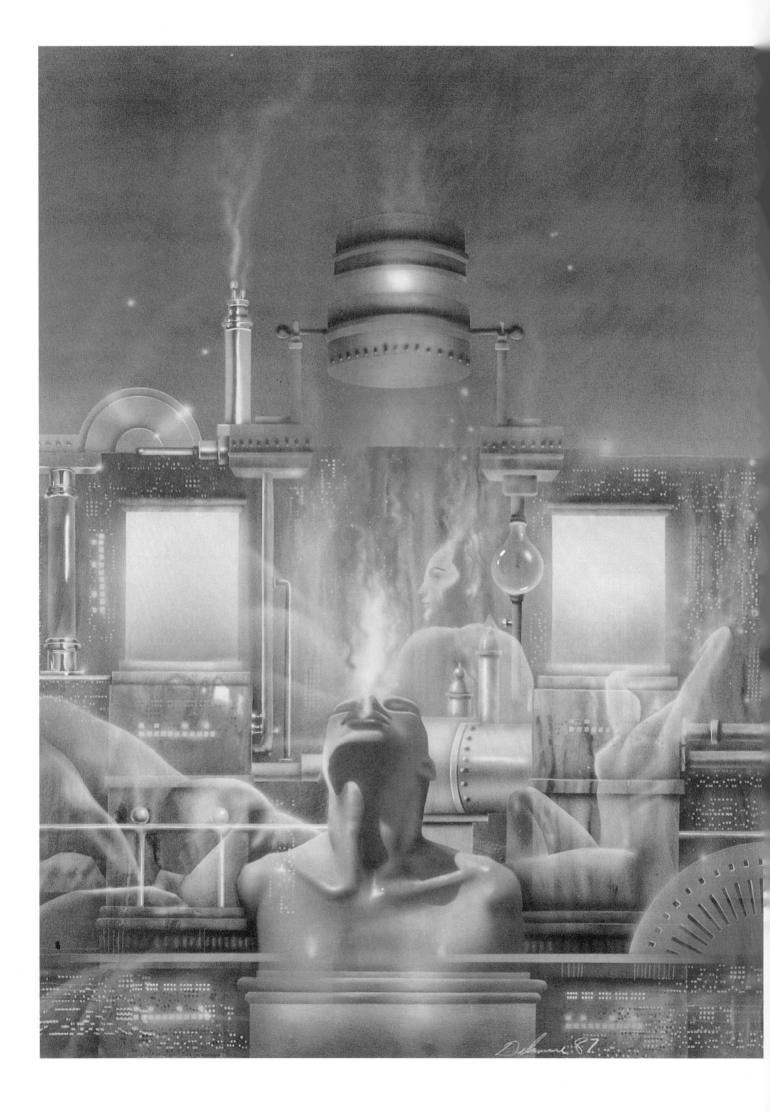

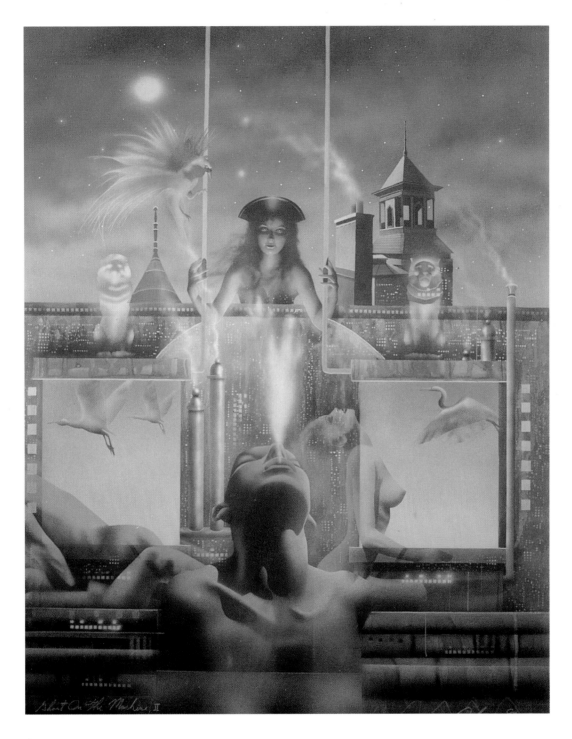

◁ **GHOST IN THE MACHINE** 1982
Gouache 18 x 24in (45 x 60cm)

△ **GHOST IN THE MACHINE II** 1989
Gouache 20 x 24in (50 x 60cm)
Delamare has always been fascinated
by Victorian theories about ether – not
the anaesthetic, but the hypothetical
substance once believed to permeate
space and act as a medium for electro-
magnetic and psychic rays. There is an
analogy here with the imagination –
ideas floating around in space waiting

to be tapped into. Similarly, he is fascinated by what lies behind the
atmospheric quality of many paintings. His aim is to make the atmosphere – the humidity, smokiness or
whatever – palpable.

▷ ▷ **EAST OF THE MOON** 1989
Gouache 20 x 35in (50 x 87cm)
A travelling caravan of players, as in
Hamlet, living in an insulated world,
which is distinctly different from the
prevailing status quo, a world of constant flux. In a different age this is the
kind of life Delamare would have chosen. There is an echo in this painting
of the Victorian photographer
Eadweard Muybridge's sequential
images of people and animals in
action, which Delamare loves.

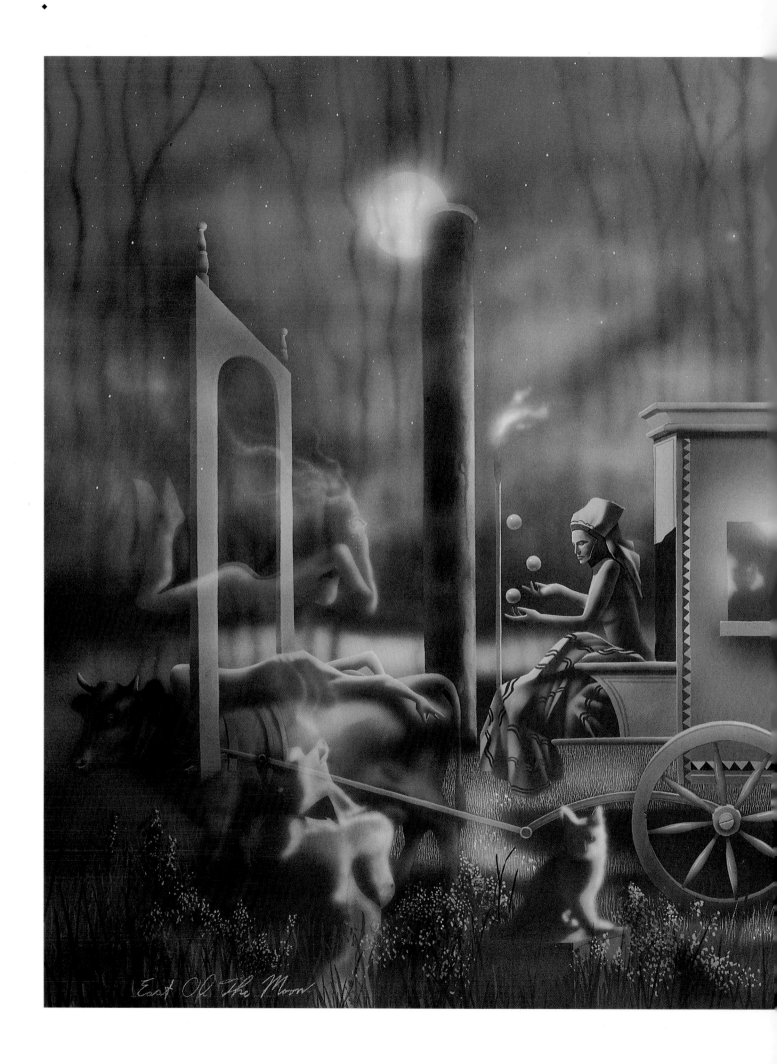

East Of The Moon

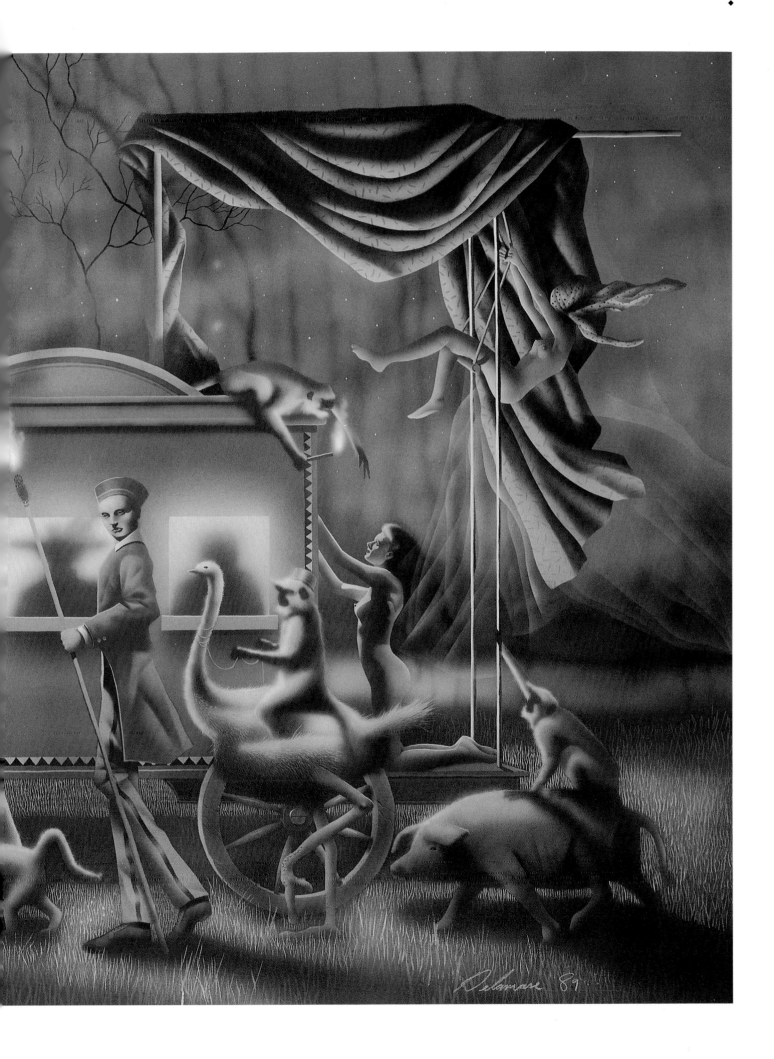

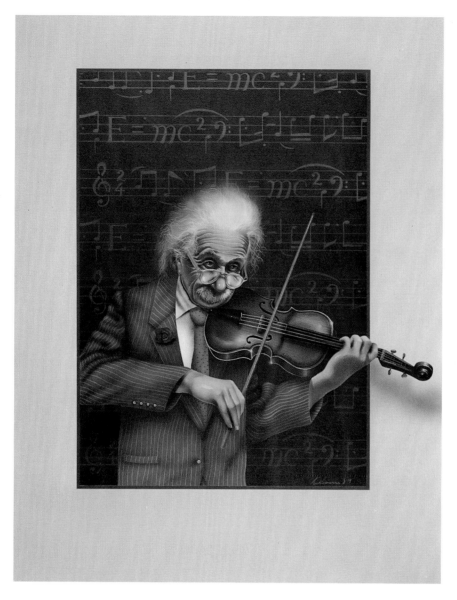

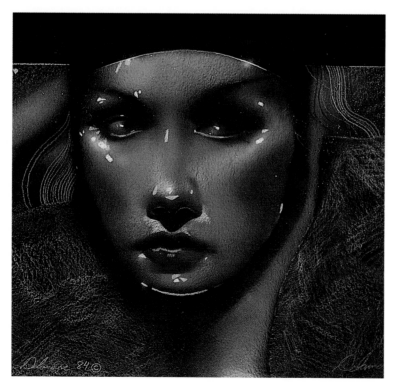

◁ **EINSTEIN** 1984

Gouache 18 x 24in (45 x 60cm)

This painting was an entry for a competition held by the Oregon Art Museum. Delamare has always loved Einstein's face, and aimed here to portray him as an artist more than a scientist, on the basis of his statement: 'Imagination is more important than knowledge.' The background shows the famous formula converted into music, which is not implausible given that Einstein enjoyed playing the violin.

▷ **JOAN** 1984

Mixed media 8 x 10in (20 x 25cm)

Portrait of an actress friend, hence the mask-like quality of her features and the suggestion of stage lights sparkling on her skin.

▷ **TROPICAL** 1987

Gouache 18 x 24in (45 x 60cm)

The title was suggested by the hint of tropical growth in the background. The picture also reflects Delamare's love of archaic machinery (particularly in this case 1940s' hair dryers), and its scale in relation to humans. There is a faintly science-fiction touch in the way the machinery seems to be an extension of the person. Is Delamare interested in SF? 'On the whole I have no real feeling for it, especially not hardware-oriented fiction. I agree with Harlan Ellison when he said that the only science fiction that interests him is that which shows the human heart in conflict with itself. What I am mainly interested in is the human condition.'

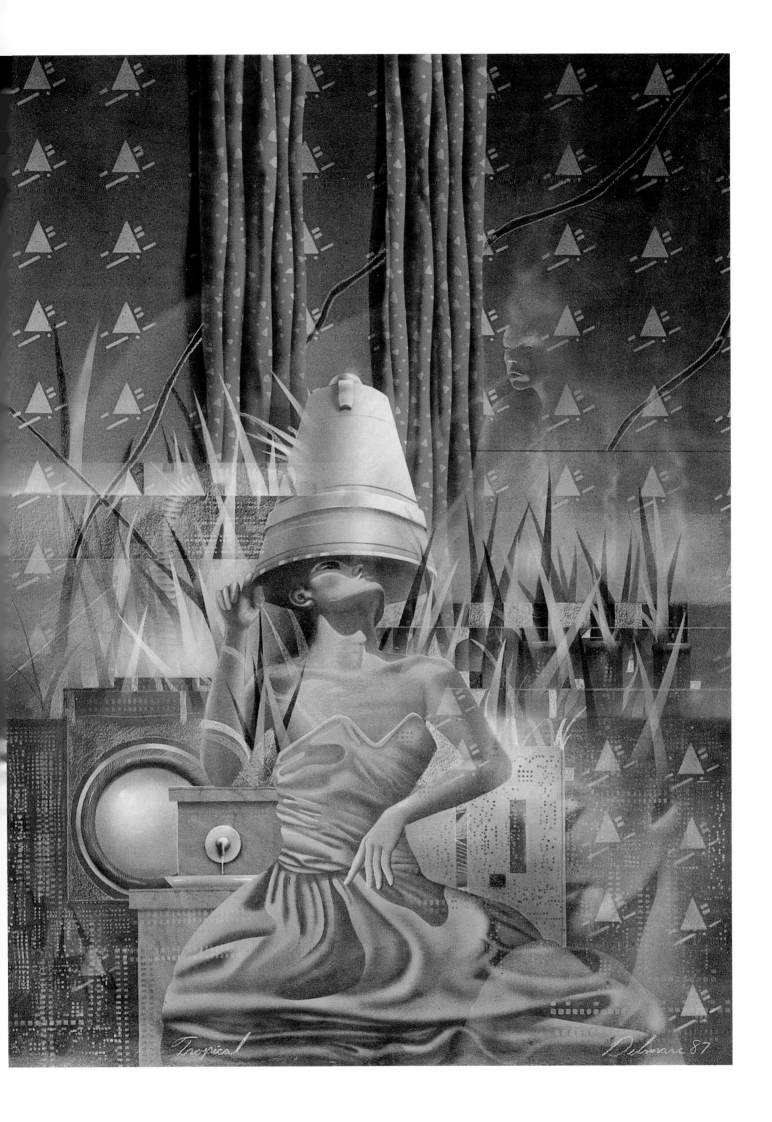

Tropical

Delaware 87

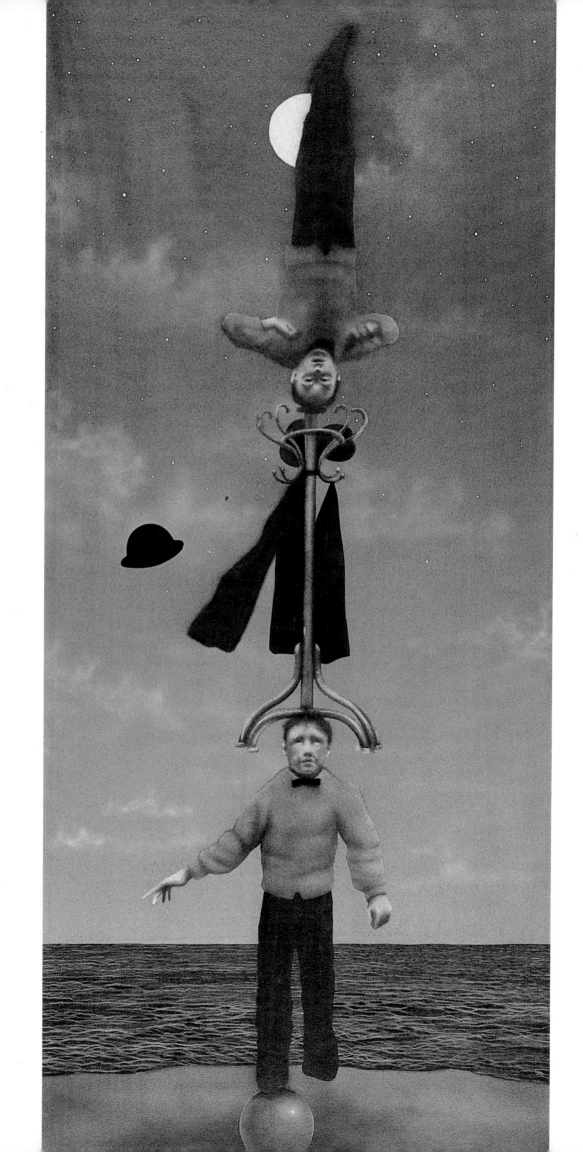

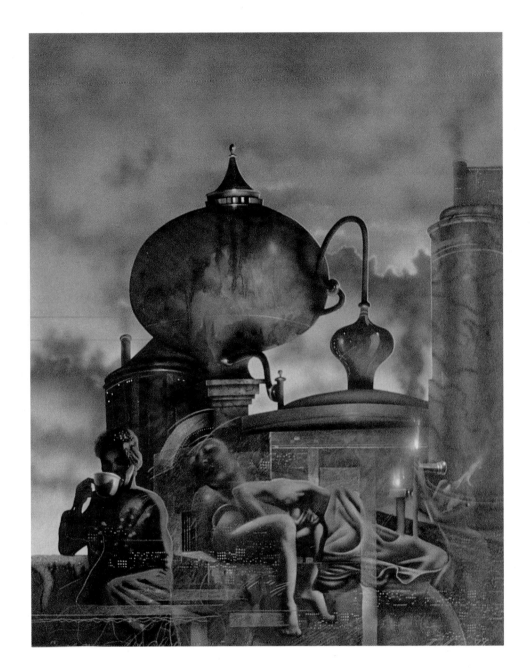

◁ **ASCENSION I** 1982

Gouache 10 x 20in (25 x 50cm)

Performers without an audience
engaged in activity for their own edi-
fication. In a roundabout way this
reminds Delamare of his favourite
playwright Samuel Beckett. The
bowler hat is a nod to René
Magritte's influence on the picture.

△ **HUNGRY LIGHTS OF PARADISE**
1988

Gouache 18 x 24in (45 x 60cm)

In the foreground a lady is mundanely
sipping tea or coffee, while everything
else is an extrapolation of what is
going on in her mind. The sombre
colours suggest loss or longing, while
the machinery is emblematic of the
constant human attempt to codify and
control life.

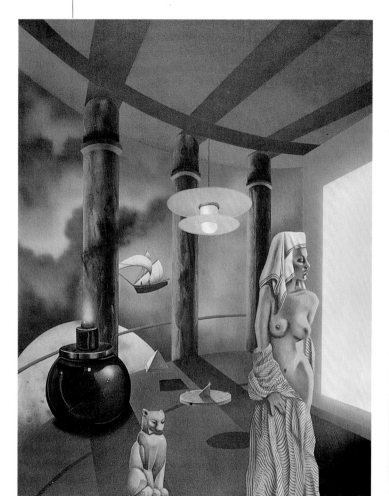

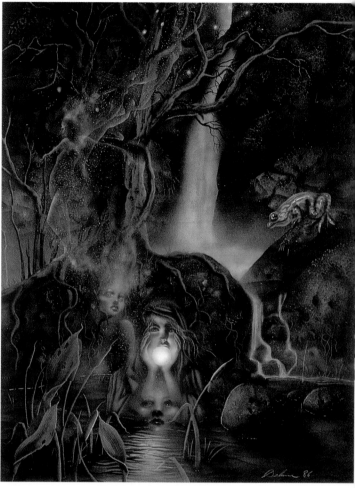

△ **PHARAOH'S CAT** 1983
Gouache 18 x 24in (45 x 60cm)

◁ **MIRANDA'S POOL** 1986
Gouache 18 x 24in (45 x 60cm)
A sample of a project Delamare hopes
to undertake one day – a picture book
version of Shakespeare's *The Tempest*,
accompanied by simplified text. Part of
the appeal is to make an act of homage
to the playwright, but the play also
contains all Delamare's favourite
elements – mermaids, spirits, monsters
and dramatic scenery – and offers
wonderful illustration potential.

▷ **TWIN CATHEDRALS** 1983
Gouache 18 x 24in (45 x 60cm)
The title concerns two basic atti-
tudes towards life, the Dionysian and
Apollonian – in other words the pur-
suit of pleasure or scholarship. They
are generally, as in the picture, seen
as mutually exclusive, but Delamare
admires both pursuits equally. The
problem is balancing the conflicting
demands or interests of each.

▷ ▷ **THE KAINE FAMILY** 1987
Gouache 20 x 30in (50 x 75cm)
One of the few portrait commissions
Delamare has accepted. It helped that
Russell Kaine is a good friend who
wanted something unusual and gave
him a free hand with the project.
Elements of the picture are all based
on fact. Kaine's mother was an avia-
tor, his father was once a carnival
barker and his wife's mother was a
Russian immigrant.

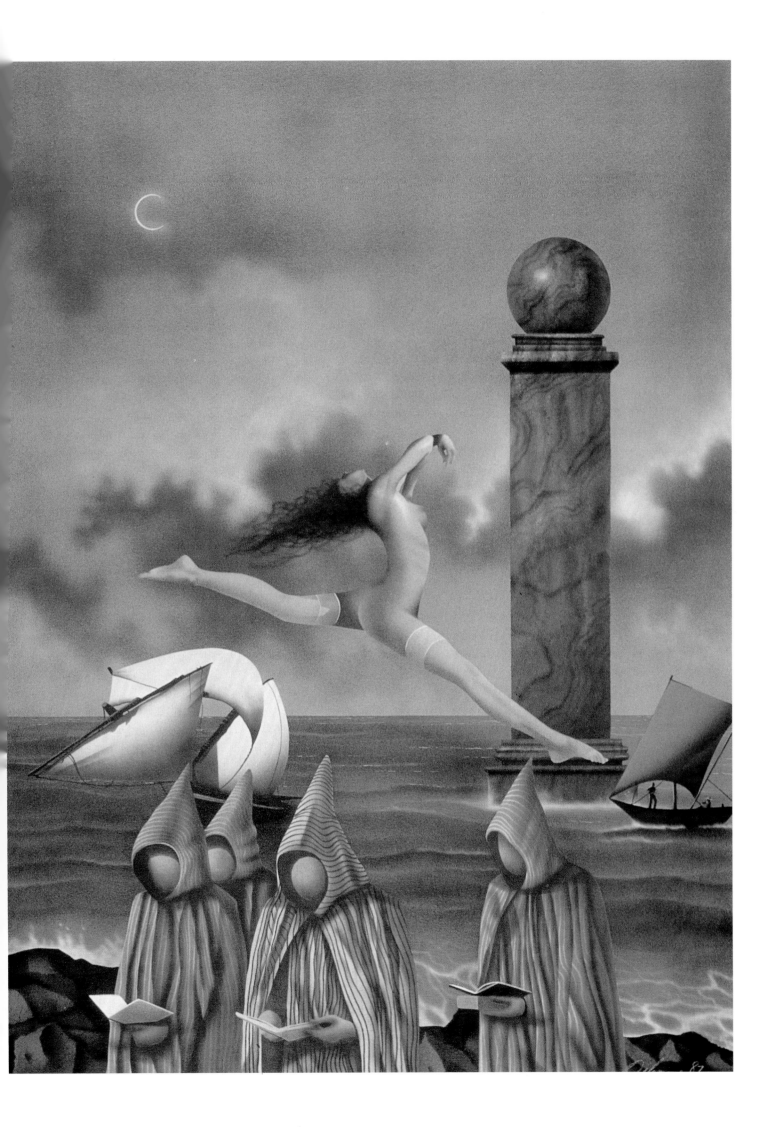

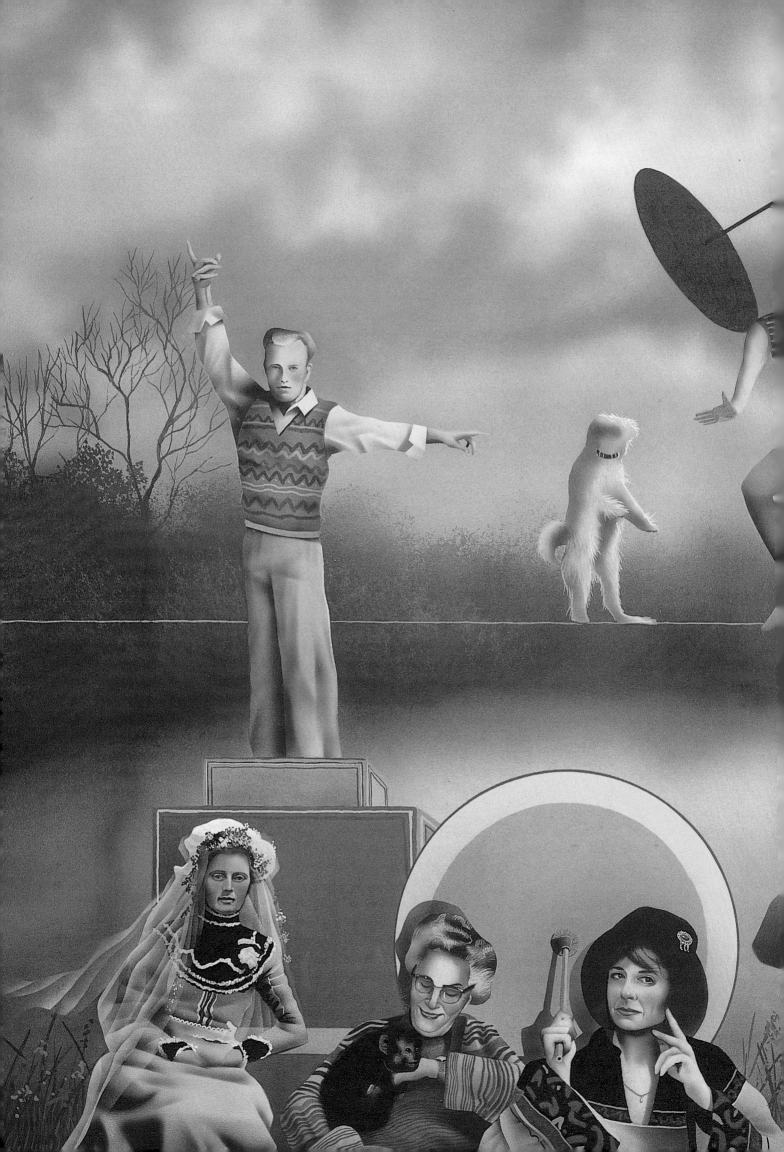

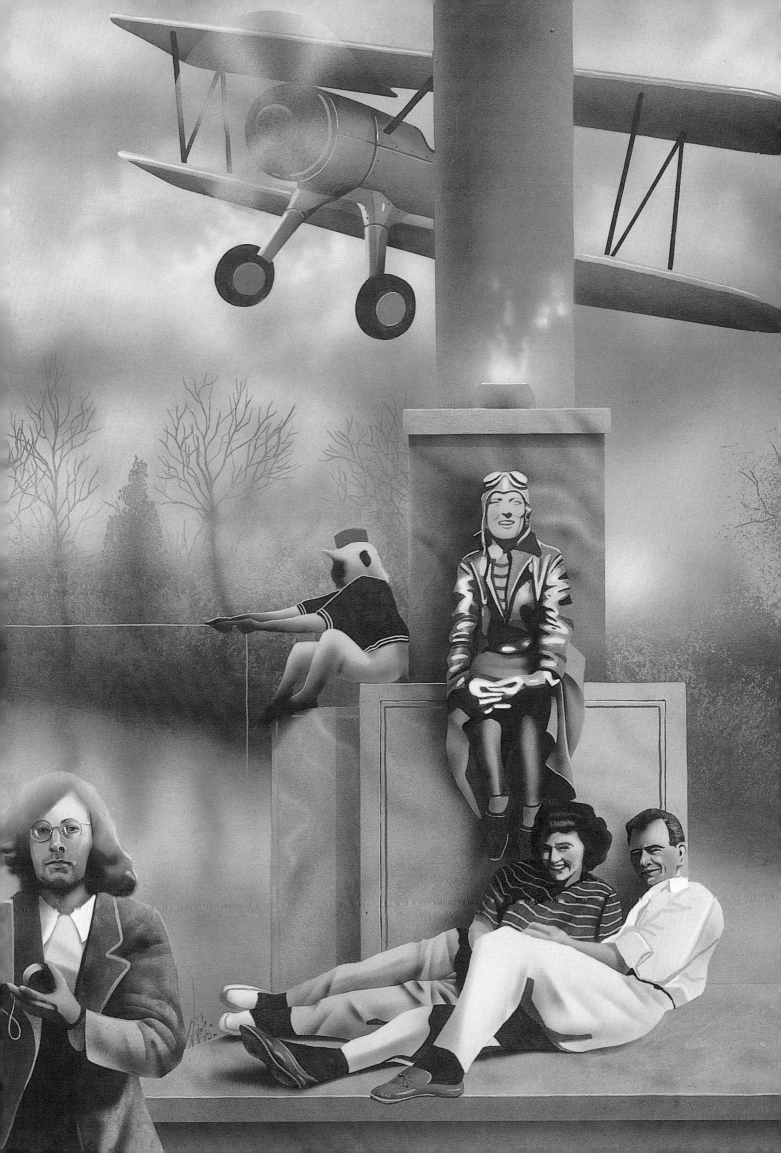

Delamare's time at college provided him with a good foundation of skills such as basic drawing and composition, but beyond that all the techniques he uses are self-taught, the result of trial and error. This was particularly the case with the airbrush. He had no interest in the instrument at college, since he had not been greatly attracted to any airbrush images he had come across. However, while using spray cans for lettering in shop windows, the potential of spraying, as an extension of his other techniques, began to dawn on him. While disliking the synthetic effect of much airbrush work, he did like the idea of smooth tone graduation and modelling form by shading, which at the time he achieved mainly by using pencil. An additional problem he faced was colouring large, plain areas such as skies in his paintings.

He began by using crude spray cans to fill in skies, and it worked terrifically. Gradually he refined the technique and progressed to using the aerosols for body tone; from that point he was inevitably on course for acquiring his first airbrush. It was a big step, undertaken with much trepidation and many mental reservations about not allowing the instrument to take over and dominate his work. Having made the step, though, he felt 'as a sculptor might after swapping a chainsaw for a dentist's instruments'. It was a great liberation and the trap of becoming an 'airbrush artist' was avoided by a conscious concentration on surface texture and detail.

There remain certain reservations about the instrument, though. Most of the art Delamare admires is by old masters such as Rembrandt, van Eyck and Caravaggio, and it feels odd trying to do the same kind of work with a tool as modern as the airbrush. Many techniques remain the same, such as underpainting and glazing (for which the airbrush is apparently 'beautiful'), and the great advantage of the airbrush is the speed with which it is possible to work. None the less, at the back of Delamare's mind lurks a feeling that he should really be working in oils, and this is a direction he is gradually taking.

In the end, though, method is not all that important: 'What counts in art is the inspiration or ideas behind it. Putting it down is probably secondary to that.' This is why he believes it is not really possible to teach art. At college he found it difficult to develop an individual approach because so much achievement was measured by how much the students' work resembled their professors'. Individual imagination was not really recognized or encouraged, but it should be possible, even if it cannot actually be taught.

What can be taught is basic technique. Delamare's own skill in drawing was developed by endless hours spent sketching driftwood, one of the professor's obsessions. In the end this exercise was worthwhile, but by the time he left college he never wanted to see another piece of driftwood again.

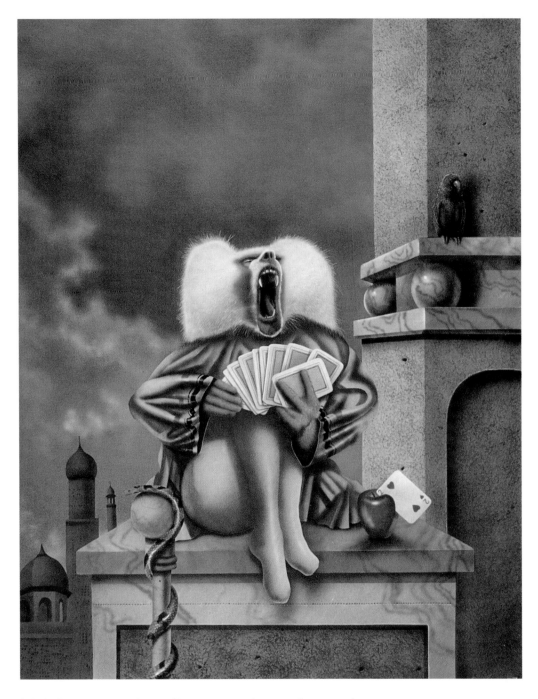

Other useful skills he acquired at college were etching and printmaking, both of which he loved – etching for its affinity with drawing, and printmaking for its physical aspect and the feeling of being linked with other printers going back to ancient times. Unfortunately, all examples of these were lost when his studio burned down, but he hopes one day to find time to do more.

For painting Delamare uses cold press illustration board because it has more texture than the hard

TWO OF HEARTS (DETAIL) 1987
Gouache 18 x 24in (45 x 57cm)
The appearance of cards in Delamare's pictures often reflect his feeling that life is pretty much like a game of chance. You can never tell when you are going to draw the ones you want.

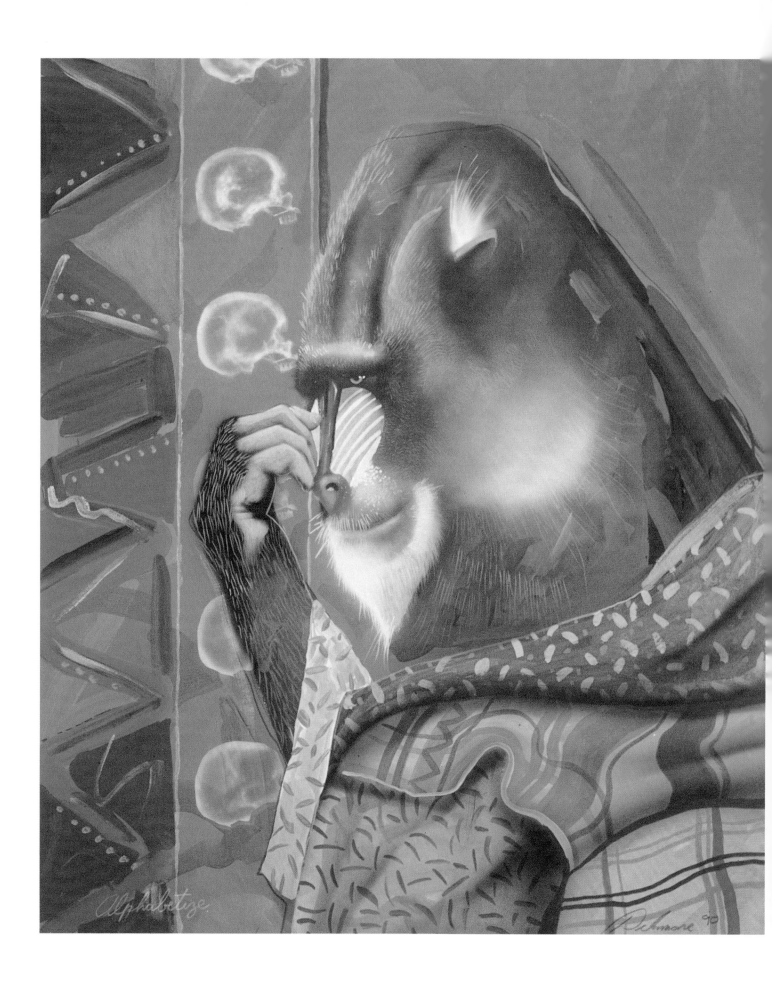

press variety commonly used by airbrush artists. If the surface is messed up a bit, all the better because spots and marks often suggest ideas and help take the intimidating edge off a completely virgin surface. Apparently, Picasso was also daunted by expensive new paper, which is one reason why he so often drew on cheap napkins or paper bags. (Another was that doodling on napkins was a great way to avoid paying restaurant bills with cash.)

The anthropomorphic pieces which follow began as a diversion but somehow managed to take over and dominate Delamare's work for several years: 'Pieces just kept coming out. It seemed there was a catalogue of things that had to be done.'

Part of the appeal can be traced back to the anthropomorphic stories he loved as a child. The full explanation he finds too complicated to put into words but it has something to do with 'a funny sort of ironic tension' that comes from the blending of human and animal qualities. Animals have characteristic temperaments we all recognize and can relate to human behaviour, so using them in pictures can be a great short cut for getting points across.

He always sees the figures as primarily human, rather than animal, and usually works from a human model: 'What I do is have people set up a pose which feels like the animal's, then do a sort of cross-version of the animal and the pose and try to get it to a point where it is plausible.' For details of the animals he keeps a resource library of magazines and photographs.

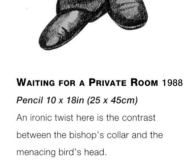

WAITING FOR A PRIVATE ROOM 1988
Pencil 10 x 18in (25 x 45cm)
An ironic twist here is the contrast between the bishop's collar and the menacing bird's head.

◁ **ALPHABETIZE** 1990
Acrylic 20 x 26in (50 x 65cm)
This picture was bought by a Portland restaurant owner, and it hangs over the table Delamare and his partner use when they go there for dinner. The creature is musing about the wonder of our alphabet, which with twenty-six characters is able to encompass all human thought and culture.

What began as a side-line diversion, not only dominated Delamare's work for a time, but proved very popular with galleries and publishing houses, happily confirming his belief that 'if you simply follow your heart, then doors begin to open'.

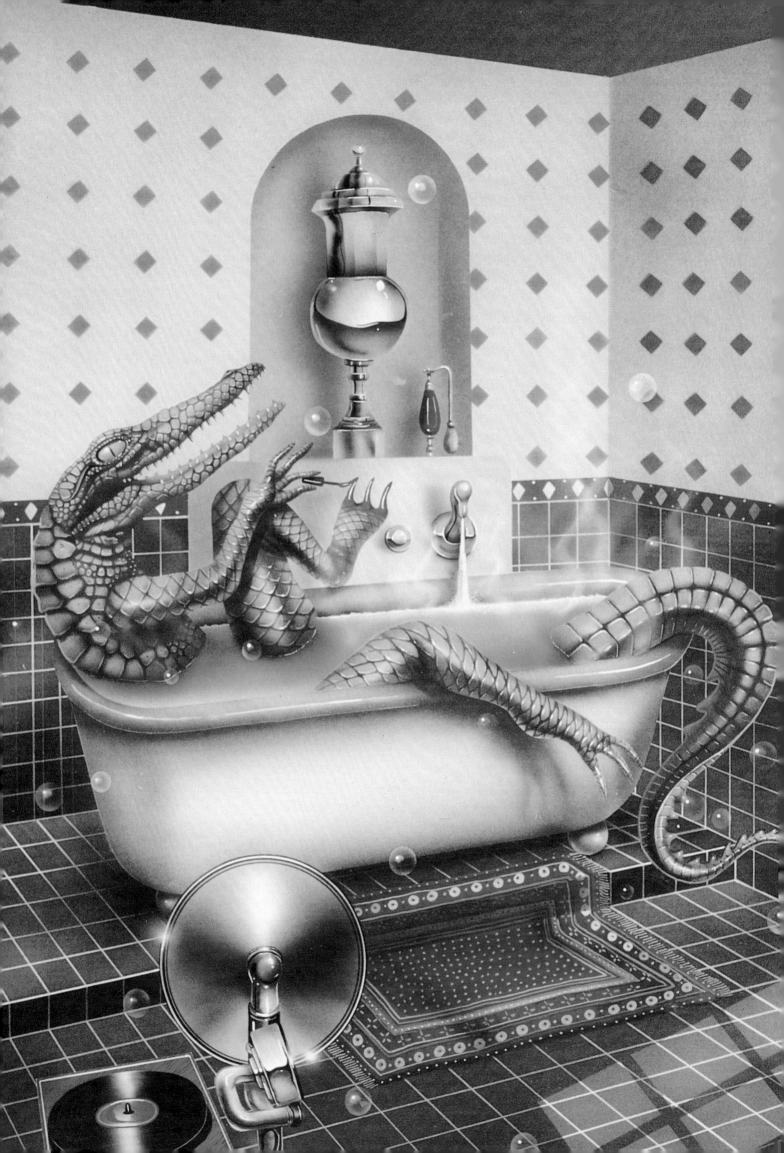

◁ **THE BATH** 1988

Gouache 18 x 24in (45 x 57cm)

Used as a commemorative poster for
the Graystone Gallery in Portland,
which is one of the main retail outlets
for Delamare's work. Often the criteri-
on for doing an anthropological piece
is thinking of the most implausible
situation the animal might find itself in,
though in this case it is more the mood
that conflicts with the creature's
naturally vicious and inhuman
temperament.

▷ **THE REED OF THE MILKY WAY**
1988

Gouache 18 x 24in (45 x 57cm)

Used as a poster for the annual busi-
ness association fête on the street
where Delamare lives. His pictures
often contain the seeds of other pictures or, as in this case, whole new
projects. This picture led to a similar
one with different characters, which in
turn led to a whole book entitled *The
Man in the Moon* and the *Air Balloon*
for which he has a series of finished
sketches awaiting painting and a
whole set of accompanying rhymes.
To get interesting angles on the air
balloon he made a model which now
hangs in his studio.

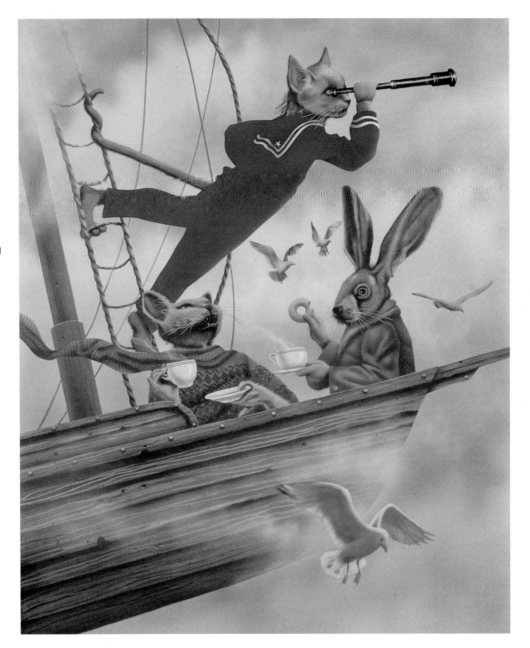

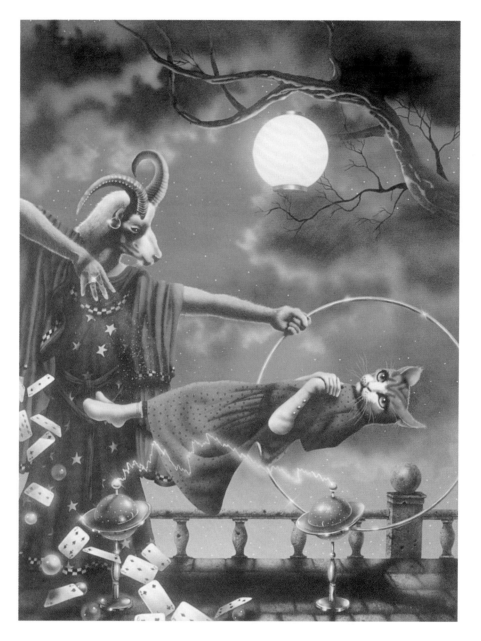

△ **THE MAGIC THEATRE** 1988
Gouache 18 x 24in (45 x 57cm)
Delamare loves magic shows. The
cascading cards were inspired by *Alice
in Wonderland*, while what at first
appears to be a moon is in fact a lamp
hanging from the tree.

▷ **THE SHADOW BOX** 1989
Acrylic 20 x 26in (50 x 65cm)
A 'wonderful metaphor' for creating
paintings, this captures how Delamare
feels when at work.

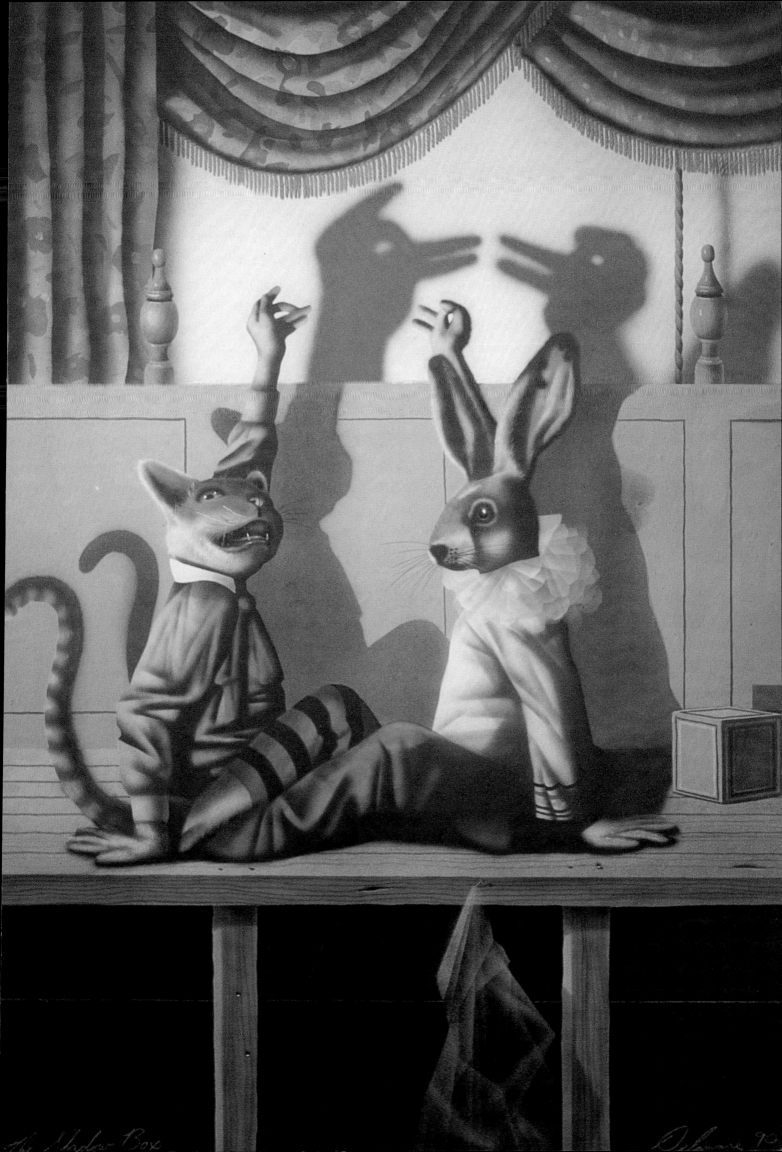

The Shadow Box

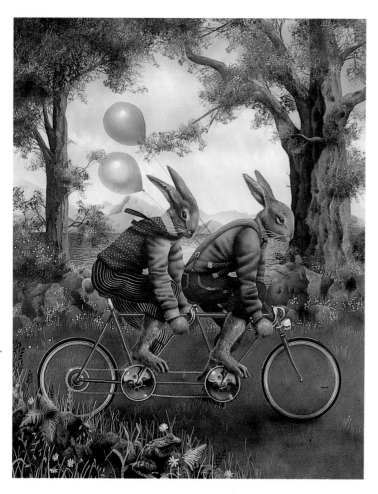

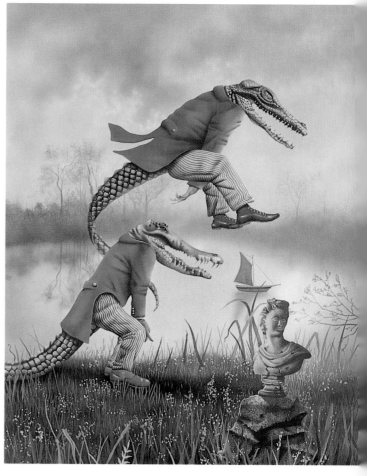

△ **BICYCLE RACE** 1985

Gouache 18 x 24in (45 x 57cm)

Compositionally this is almost a grid
and a study in twos (trees, balloons
and wheels).

△ **GREAT CAESAR'S GHOST** 1988

Gouache 18 x 24in (45 x 57cm)

The title is what Delamare imagined one
of the characters to be exclaiming as he
jumps. The setting for pictures like this

are usually imaginary. Sometimes they
are created totally out of thin air, but
where necessary, photographic references are used to supply the finishing
touches.

The Bicycle Race

The toyshop firm of Kipperbang
To celebrate four score
Decided on a challenge cup
A race from shore to shore

Each team would fly two air balloons
To trail above their heads
The canines picked their favorite – green
The rabbits' choice was red

Besides the fame and fortune
And the eighteen-karat gold
The prize included
Two weeks stay at Hotel Marigold
A trampoline, a fishing pole
A weekend movie pass
A leather-bound edition – signed –
Of Through the Looking Glass
A pocketwatch, a sailing boat
A miniature machine
And what's more
There's a year's supply
Of Tandem magazine

As daybreak broke
The finish line was coming into view
The rabbits crossed at six o'clock
The canines six o' two

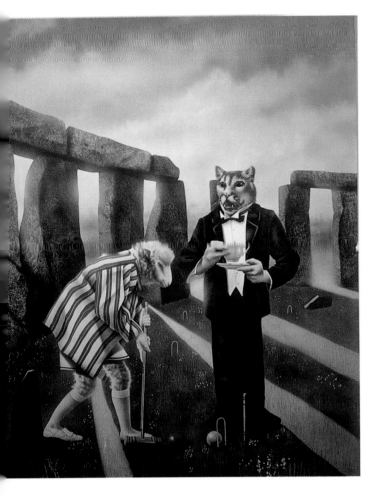

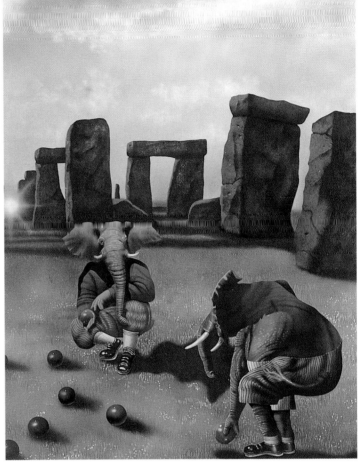

△ **THE ENTIRETY OF THE THING**

1989 *Acrylic 20 x 26in (50 x 65cm)*

The wonderfully portentous title here means...well, whatever you care to make of it really. The animals chosen for the characters are significant in these anthropomorphic pieces. Here we have a natural predator and prey

playing together, the twist being that the sheep is vanquishing the slightly startled bobcat at croquet. In a way, the picture represents the triumph of English propriety over natural instinct. What the cat would really like to do is bite the sheep's head off, but of course he won't.

Λ **THE GRAND BOWLING GREEN**

1988

Acrylic 18 x 24in (45 x 60cm)

The Grand Bowling Green

Every year like clockwork, never fail
Regardless of the weather
The elephants return to bowl
Green fields and English heather

They've never missed a bowling tryst
In well, I can't recall
I've seen them play in snowy white
I've seen them play in Fall

In summer you might see them dressed
Without a shirt or hat
They're rather large
But I must say
They both move just like cats

The games' afoot!
They cry aloud
So shoot and please don't forfeit
He cinches up his trousers
And the globes spin into orbit

TEETER TOTTER 1988

Gouache 20 x 26in (50 x 65cm)

A whimsical idyll into which more can perhaps be read. The lion, as a natural aggressor, is roaring with frustration at being suspended in mid-air by the elephant. On a playful level many of these pictures show animals subverting primal antagonisms by almost human cunning.

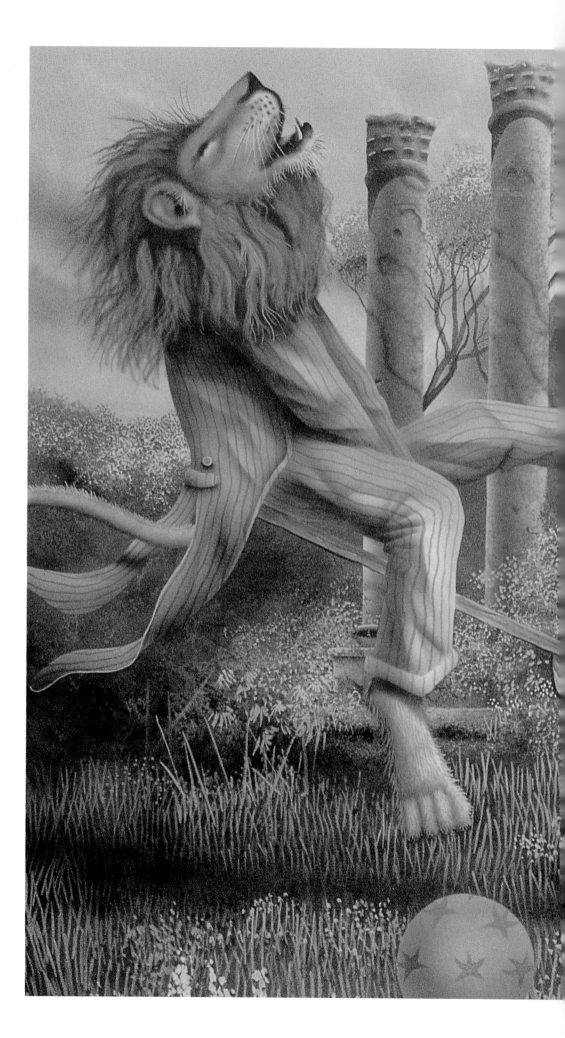

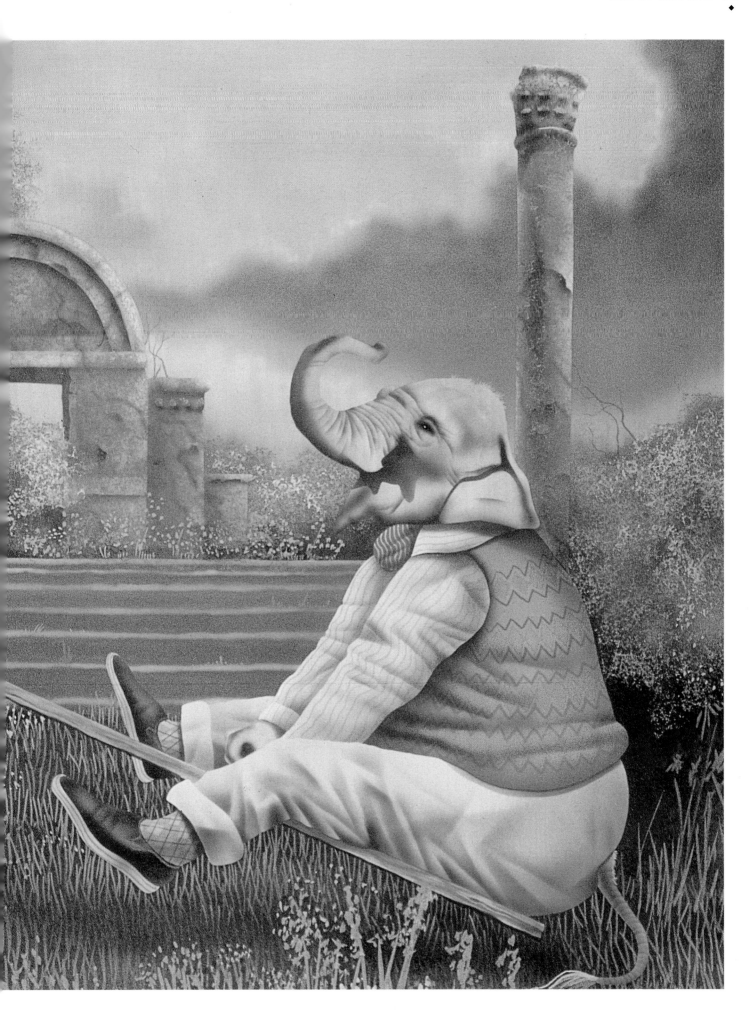

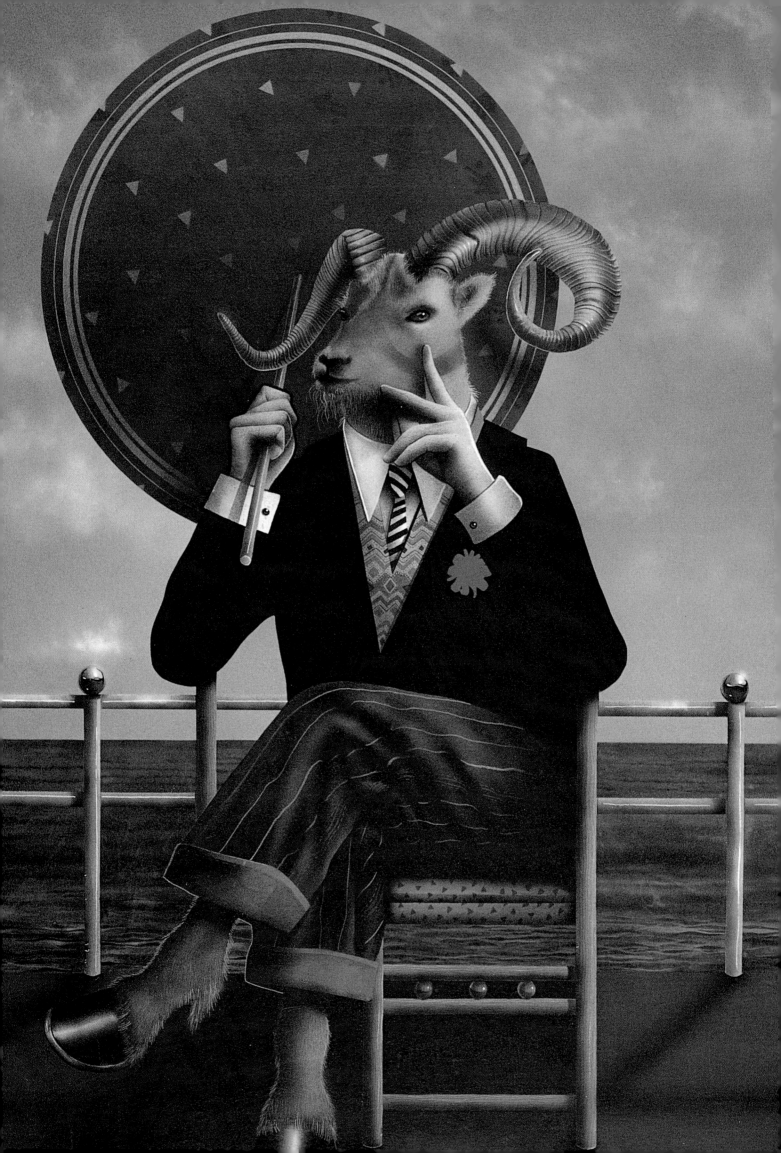

The Winter's Tale

When December spreads its winter coat
Of this it can be said
All of the bears excepting two
Retire to their beds

For Beatrice and her Danny meet
Each year when all is white
On frozen lakes they pirouette
Under the clear moonlight

And in that white arena
With its silent serenade
The only sound for miles and miles
The hiss of silver blades

When springtime's breeze
Touches the trees
And lakes and rivers flow
They sleep away the summer days
In dreams of winter snow

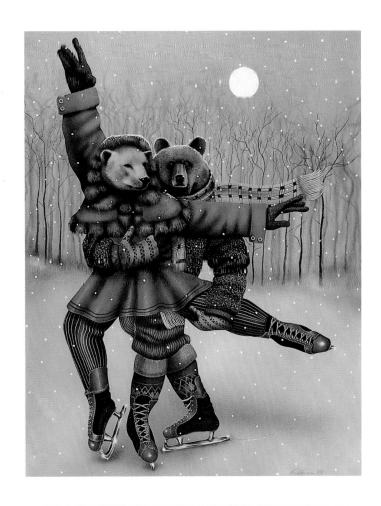

◁ **THE CRUISE** 1986

Gouache 18 x 24in (45 x 60cm)

Delamare loves photographs which date from the turn of the century and has a fair collection. Because of the length of exposure they often contain an interesting contradiction; casual poses are rigidly held for the sake of the camera. This picture is derived from one such photograph.

▷ **THE JITTERBUG** 1988

20 x 26in (50 x 65cm)

The glowing jukebox is probably one of the ultimate Art Deco creations. This picture derived from a book about them, which was given to Delamare by a friend who actually owned one of the beauties.

◁ **THE WINTER'S TALE** 1984

Gouache 18 x 24in (45 x 60cm)

Most of Delamare's compositions feature individuals or couples, a reflection of his personal disinclination for crowds. On the whole, he prefers his own company or interaction with just one other person. This picture also reflects his love of snow. It does not snow as much as he would like in Portland, especially not at Christmas, but a ready solution is only an hour's journey away in the mountains to the east.

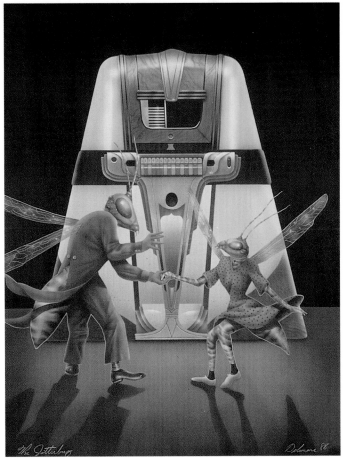

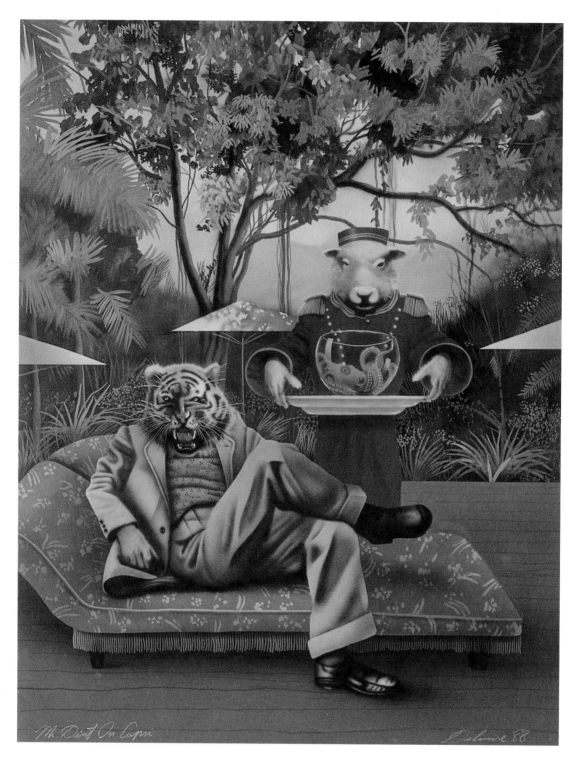

△ **MR DINT IN CAPRI** 1988
Gouache 18 x 24in (45 x 60cm)
The tiger's vacation is about to be
undermined by something unsavoury
being served up to him by the cheeky
bellhop.

▷ **SONGS FOR SUPPER** 1985
Gouache 18 x 24in (45 x 60cm)
A wry contrast is drawn here with the
reality of normal cats yowling under
the moon for food. Delamare feels a
great warmth towards street musicians
who improvise a living outside the
system.

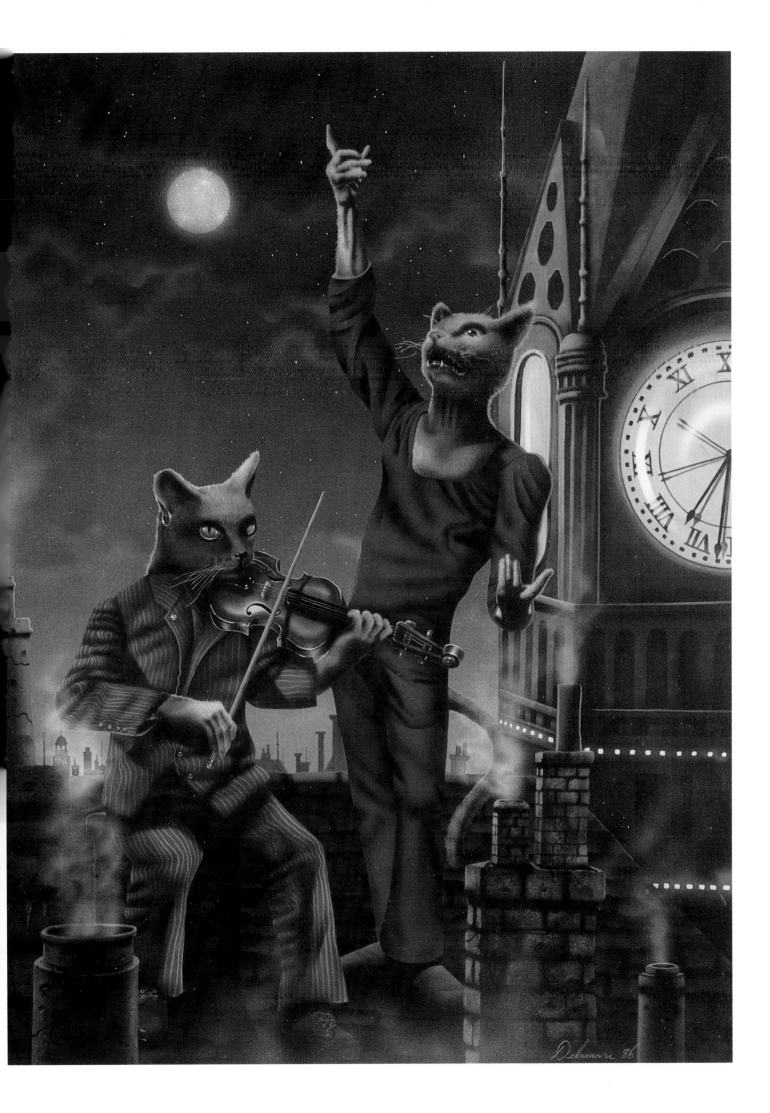

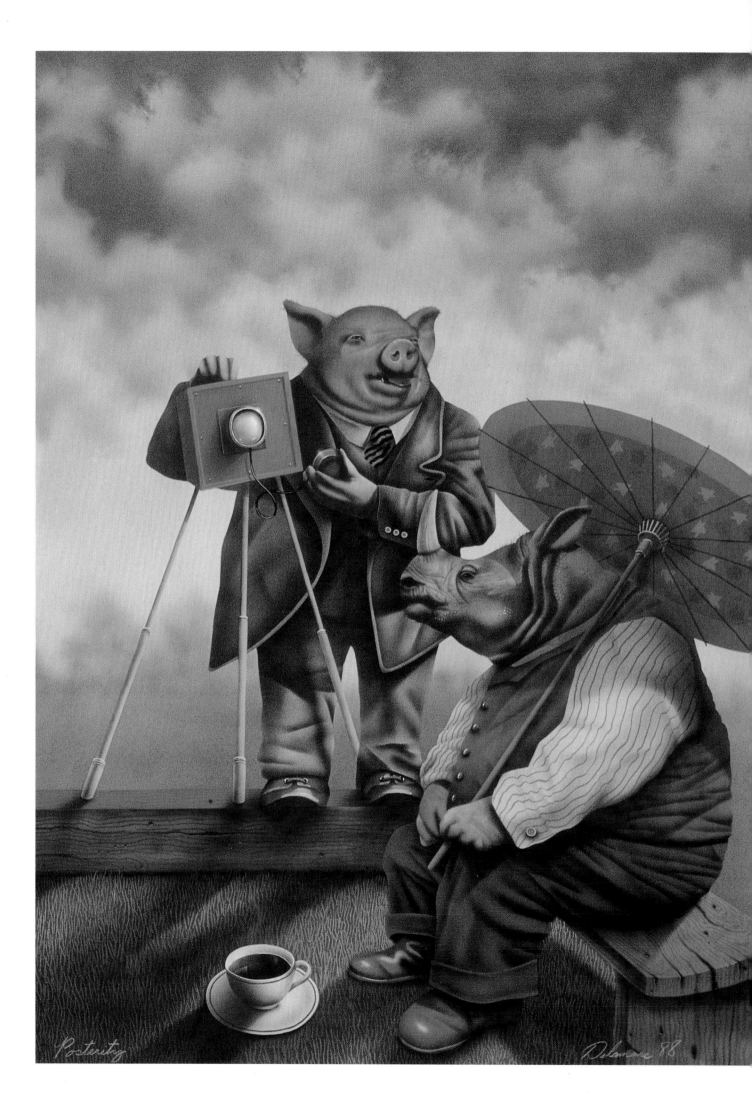

Posterity

Delaune 88

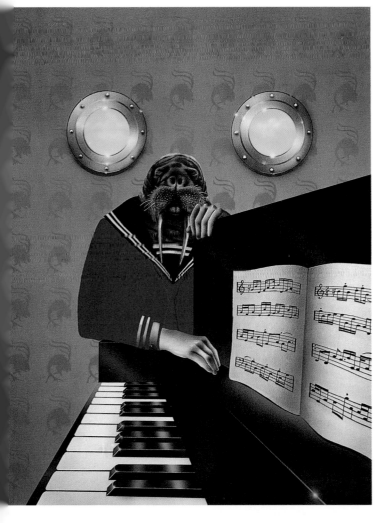

◁◁ **POSTERITY** 1988

Gouache 20 x 26in (50 x 65cm)

Inspired by a wonderful Goya painting of an aristocratic family, whose main common feature was incredible ugliness. Delamare marvels that they should have wanted themselves immortalized in the first place, and have paid good money to be so unflattered.

◁ **CONCERTO AT SEA** 1987

Gouache 16 x 20in (40 x 50cm)

For those who are slow with puns, there is one in the title. The original version of this was an early portrait of Count Basie in the same pose.

▷ **COMPTON GLOBE** 1985

Gouache 16 x 20in (40 x 50cm)

Essentially a portrait of Delamare himself first thing in the morning. The animal association is with the rabbit in *Alice in Wonderland*. Though he liked the pictures, the book was not a particular favourite of his as a child, but it is now, and he has several different editions. Would he like to have a go at illustrating it himself? 'I would certainly take the challenge if someone asked me, but I wonder if I could bring anything new to the subject. Can anyone improve on Tenniel?'

▽ **M** 1988

Gouache 20 x 26in (50 x 65cm)

Being a 'terrible buff', Delamare gets a lot of inspiration from films. This picture is a humorous take-off of a film noire of the same title in which a murderer is caught in the act and has an M painted on his back as he tries to flee the scene. Here one can see a similar mark reflected in the glass, and on the tails of mice protruding from the mouth and pocket of the culprit.

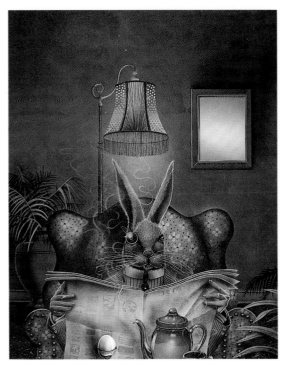

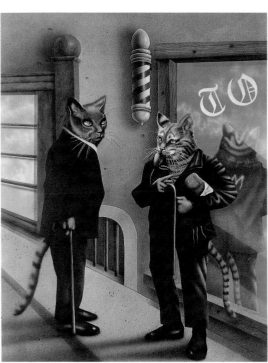

Monkeys (using the term in its broadest sense) often crop up in Delamare's paintings looking grave and thoughtful as they gaze upon the human activity around them. What do they represent? Delamare is reluctant to go into the symbolism too deeply, quoting an Anthony Burgess saying: 'Let us not be too tempted to drag the big dream up to the light.' He is wary of demystifying his pictures too much but does reply obliquely: 'There is something about monkeys being very close to humans but having more of the primal urges than we do. I often think there is a closer parallel between humans and monkeys than is generally recognized. After all, we do share something like 90 per cent of the same genes but we see monkeys as just animals. We believe we have a superior system for working out all the problems of life but maybe this is an illusion? We can organize the bits and pieces perhaps, but too often we're engaged in making up problems in the field of our understanding as a kind of distraction because we know we cannot solve the real problems of life. So perhaps we are not so far removed from monkeys because most of our cleverness is self-absorbed or self-defeating. We live in a supposedly rational, Newtonian world, but we are not really satisfied with it. Not enough to console ourselves.'

Humans are so obviously different in behaviour to their closest biological relatives, the key possibly being our ability to extract and pass on information, but does it follow that we are superior to the same degree? That is possibly the question his quizzical monkeys are posing. However busily we occupy ourselves with the intellectual pursuits peculiar to humans, the primal side of our nature refuses to go away.

One of Delamare's ongoing interests is observing how people balance the animal side of their nature with the rest. Sometimes, as perhaps with the screaming monkey which recurs in several pictures, he considers the need to keep the beast in check. More often, however, his monkeys seem to assert the importance of animal instinct and the dignity of the beast.

He is not alone in his views about monkeys. The Great Ape Project, launched in London recently with the support of many writers and heavyweight academics, has as its aim the extension of human rights to all apes on biological, philosophical and ethical grounds. The project's founder, Peter Singer, professor of bioethics at Monash University in Australia, argues that the great apes' mental and emotional capacities justify their inclusion in a 'community of equals' with humans.

In support of this case is quoted the example of Koko, a twenty-year-old lowland gorilla living at the Gorilla Foundation in Woodside, California. This creature has not only learned a thousand words of American Sign Language, but has invented sign words of her own and can understand several thousand words of spoken English, being able to respond to questions in phrases of up to four words. She also enjoys painting and drawing, telling jokes and reminiscing about the past.

On the biological front, chimpanzees' closest relatives are not other monkeys but humans, with whom they share an astonishing 98.4 per cent of their DNA. In fact, molecular biologists calculate that we are both descended from a common ancestor that lived in Africa some five to seven million years ago.

Given his fascination with monkeys, has Delamare ever kept one? No, but he would happily take one off someone's hands if it needed a home. The closest he has ever come to it was once acquiring a quadraplegic opossum from an animal sanctuary. Dubbed Stinky, it was 'a sweet animal with an opposable thumb and a wonderful tail'. Unfortunately, Stinky never quite came to terms with the resident cats and had to go. Apart from the loss of so delightful a pet, Delamare has a lingering regret that he never painted the creature while it was with him.

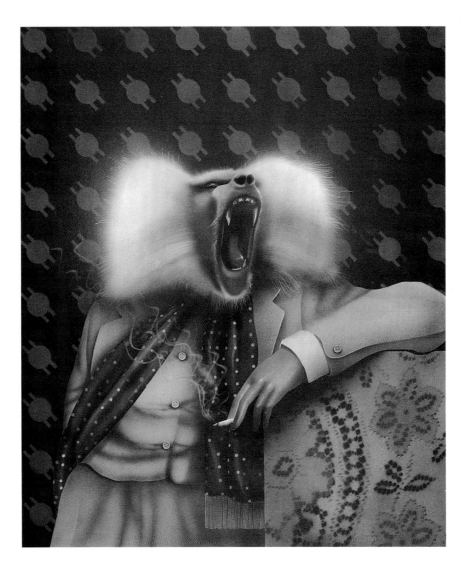

HARLOW'S MONKEY 1984

Gouache 18 x 24in (45 x 60cm)

A lovely incongruity here between the rakish pose and bizarre expression. The title was suggested by the 1930s' feel of the background, which called to mind Jean Harlow. This is perhaps an unsuccessful suitor.

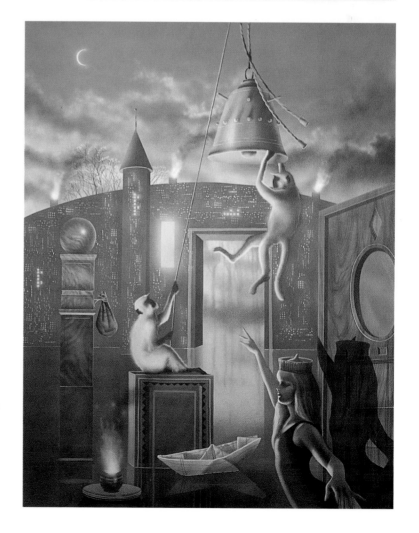

◁ THE EXCURSION 1987

Gouache 18 x 24in (45 x 60cm)

This reflects a fondness Delamare has for topiary gardens and mazes. The greenery is shaped rather like the bow of a boat, which gives the feel that it is heading out towards some distant horizon.

▷ SENSORIUM 1990

Gouache 20 x 26in (50 x 65cm)

One of Delamare's favourite pieces, with elements which have surfaced in projects such as *The Tin Soldier* and *Cinderella*. The strong atmospheric quality and mood of anticipation owe much to the Metaphysical school of art, of whom de Chirico is a particular favourite. The scene teeters on the brink of change – a bell is about to ring, night is about to fall and the figure in the foreground is pregnant with possibilities, but we are given no clue as to what they might be.

▷ ▷ THE LATE SHOW 1989

Gouache 20 x 26in (50 x 65cm)

A quite literal stage show which might well be performed by the travelling company in East of the Moon (see pp. 52-3). Included is a portrait of one of Delamare's own cats, who has a habit of sleeping in flowerpots.

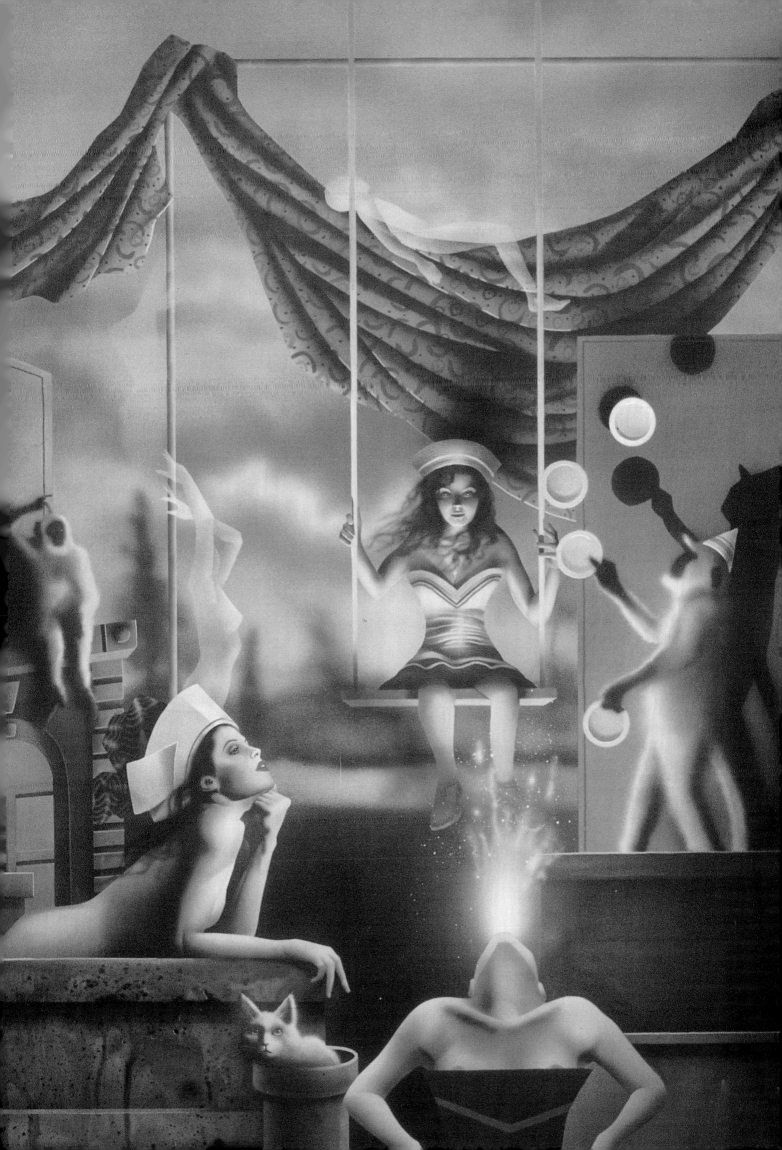

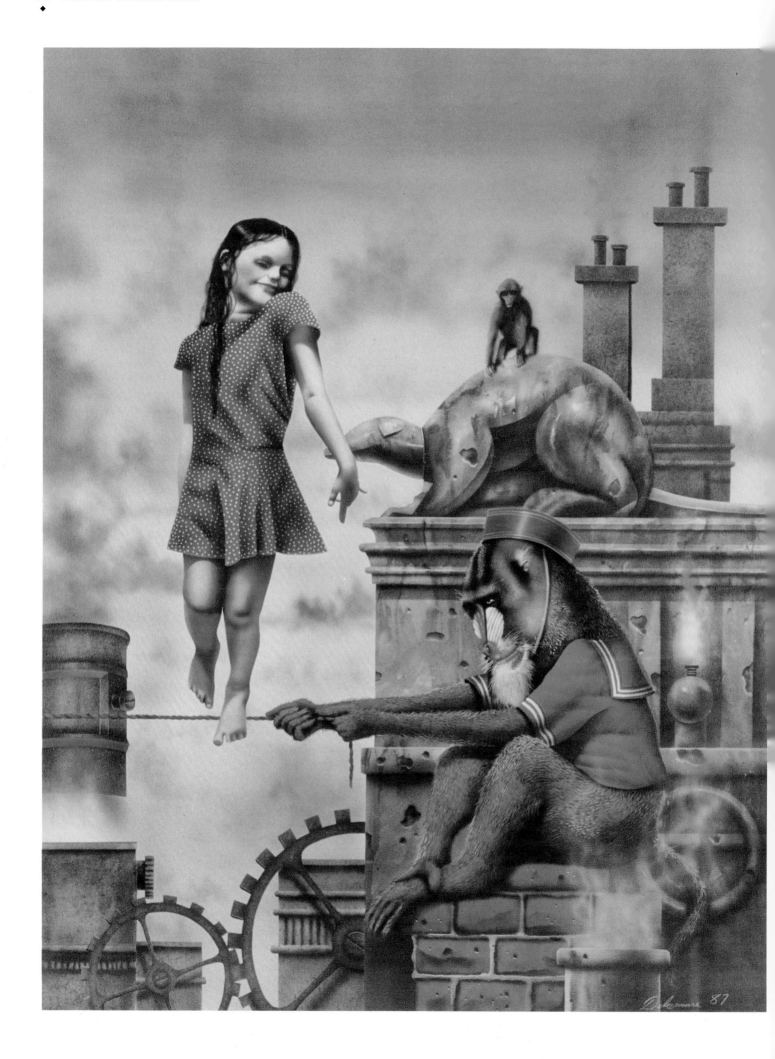

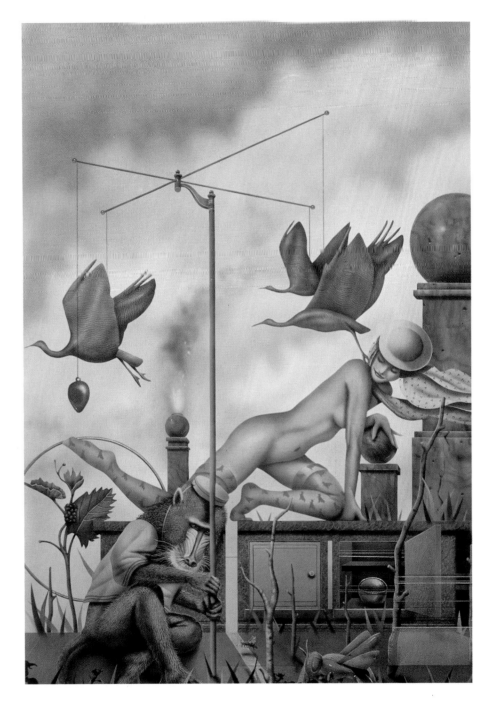

◁ **EURYDICE** 1983
Gouache 18 x 24in (45 x 60cm)

△ **THE BEEKEEPER** 1988
Gouache 18 x 24in (45 x 60cm)
Picasso once said that 'art is the lie
that allows one to see the truth'. In a
similar way Delamare has often found
that the essence of something can be
better suggested by an artificial
representation than an attempt at

naturalism – in this case a mobile of
wooden birds instead of real ones. The
picture was prompted by the film *Bliss*,
in which a man falls in unrequited love
with a beekeeper. Since she will have
nothing to do with him, he plants trees
around her property for the bees to
feed on. When she tastes the ensuing
honey she realizes what has happened
and finally accepts his love.

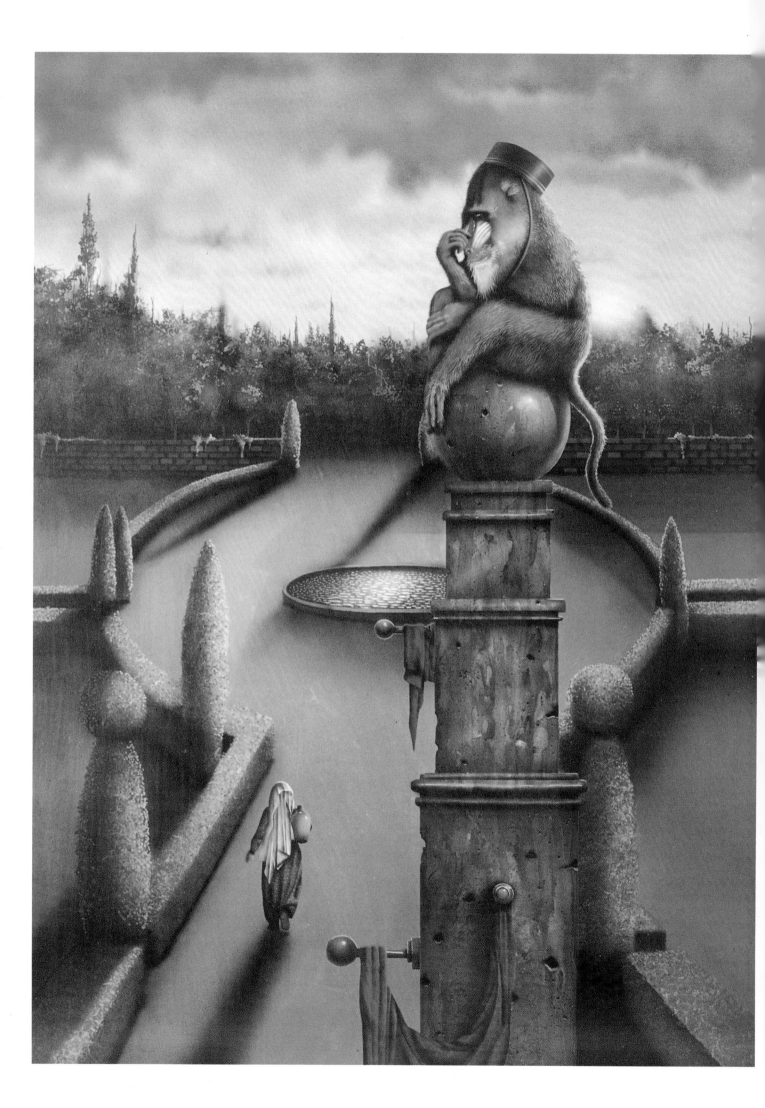

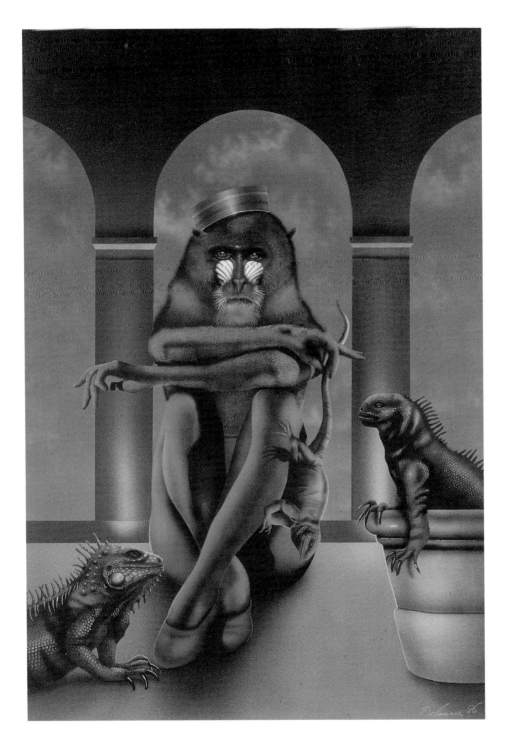

◁ **WATER FROM THE WELL** 1987
Gouache 18 x 24in (45 x 60cm)
The monkey perched on his detached
vantage point reminds Delamare a little
of himself. As is natural for an artist, he
is a great observer. He enjoys, say in a
park, watching life unfolding around
him without necessarily wanting to be
part of the action.

△ **THE LIZARD PROBLEM** 1986
Gouache 18 x 24in (45 x 60cm)
A piece for Delamare's *Creature
Comforts* book.

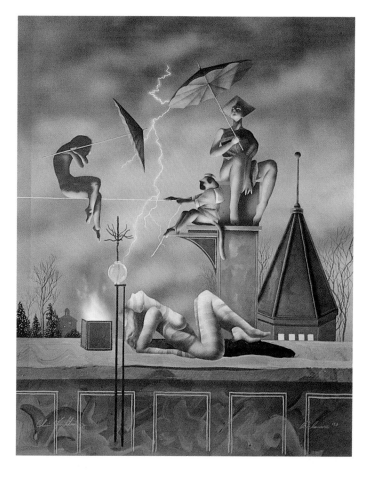

◁ **CHAIN LIGHTNING** 1990
Gouache 20 x 26in (50 x 65cm)

▷ **JINGLE-JONNIE** 1987
Gouache 20 x 26in (50 x 65cm)
When his BEEKEEPER painting was
bought at a gallery showing, Delamare
was commissioned to produce something with the same feel but different
imagery. As the client had a Russian
background, Delamare introduced
some ethnic elements. A jingle-jonnie
is an eastern European musical instrument used on parades; the bells,
which are mounted on a pole, chime
when the pole is struck on the ground.

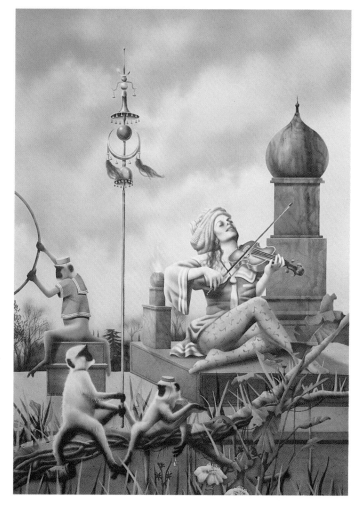

▷ **AVALON** 1990
Mixed media 20 x 26in (50 x 65cm)
Once, while musing on the subject of
the Celtic island paradise, it occurred
to Delamare that having unlimited time
on one's hands could be a burden
after a while. He wondered what
games the departed might invent to
while away eternity, and how they
were likely to become more and more
obscure, as in this one with birds on
sticks. The image of the zebra drifting
by in a boat recurred later in
Cinderella, transmuted into an elephant in a gondola. This apparently
surreal detail was, however, supplied
with a rational explanation.

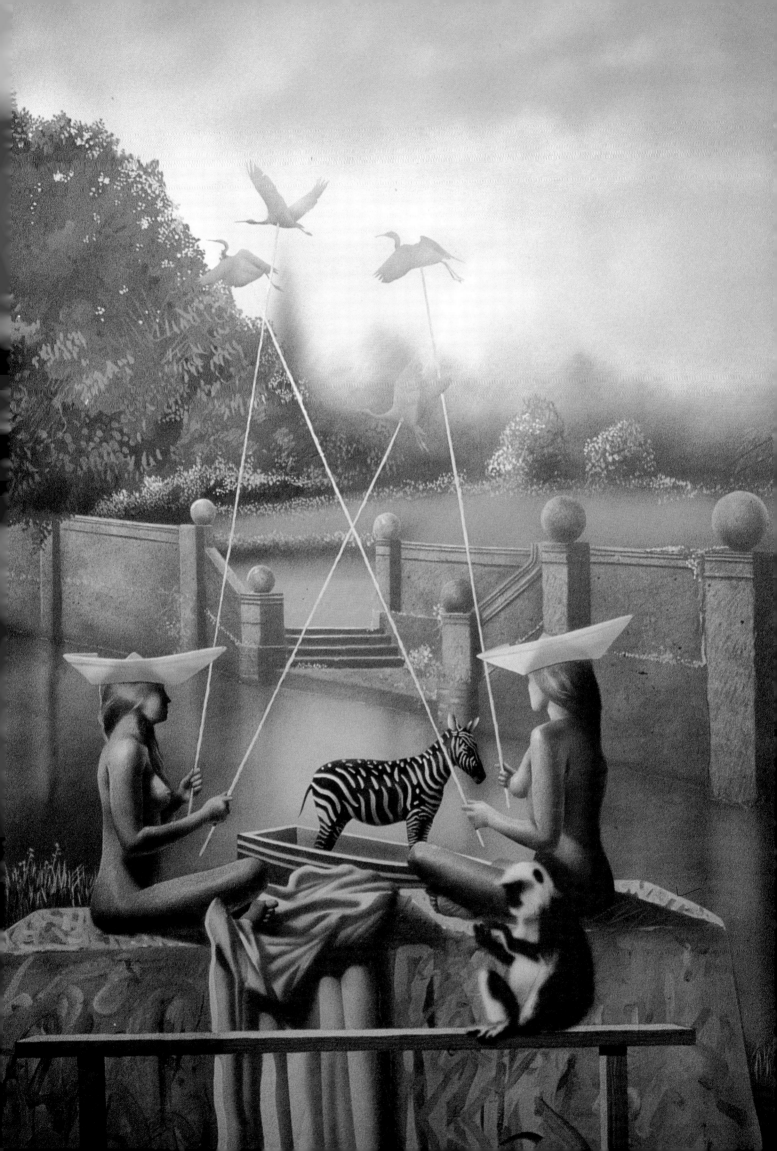

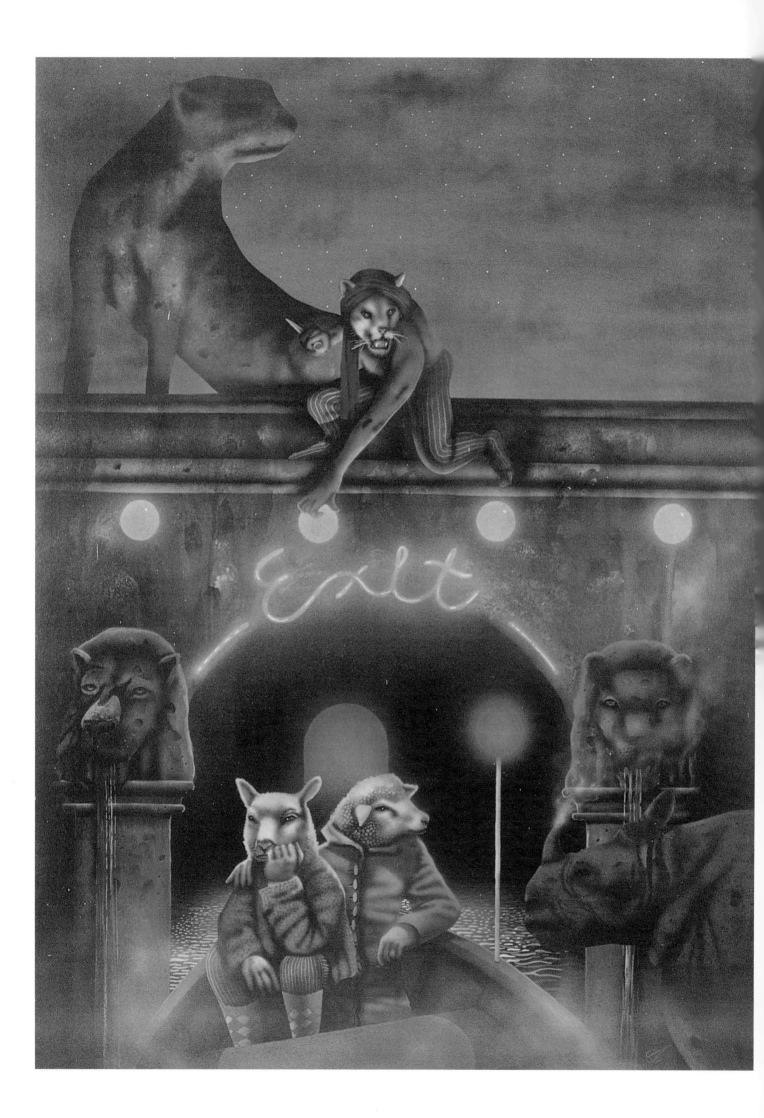

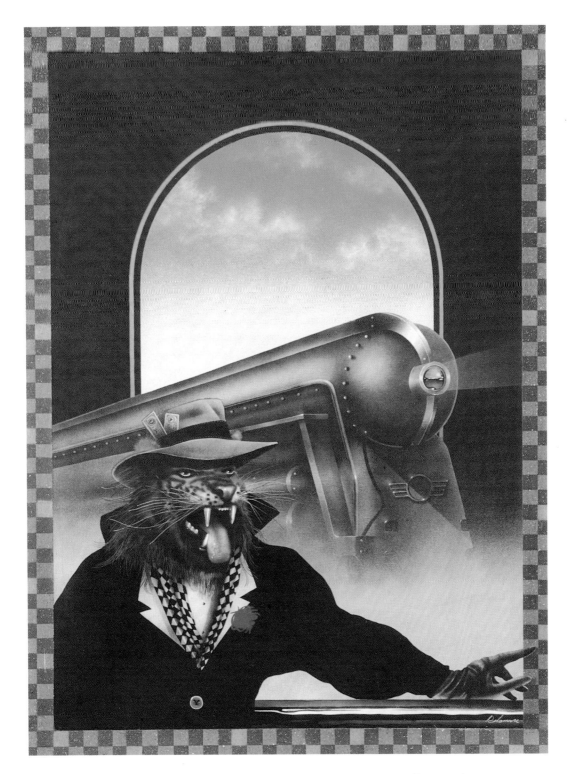

◁ **ROSENCRANTZ AND
GUILDENSTERN** 1985
Gouache 18 x 24in (45 x 60cm)
A skit on the characters in *Hamlet*
(also the subject of a Tom Stoppard
play) who are brought on and casually
despatched out of the blue like sacrifi-
cial sheep. It was also inspired by a
famous and wonderful photograph of

Sigmund Freud and Carl Jung riding
together through the tunnel of love on
Coney Island in New York in 1909. As
it turned out, this visit to the United
States marked the end of their friendly
relations.

△ **THE ORIENT EXPRESS** 1984
Gouache 16 x 20in (40 x 50cm)

▷ ▷ **PARADISE LOST** 1988
Gouache 20 x 30in (50 x 75cm)
To get a fresh approach, Delamare
invented a little compositional mind-
game. The overall feeling of the piece
is taken from Dante's classic, without
any attempt at a literal interpretation,
while the number of images matches
the number of cantos in the poem.

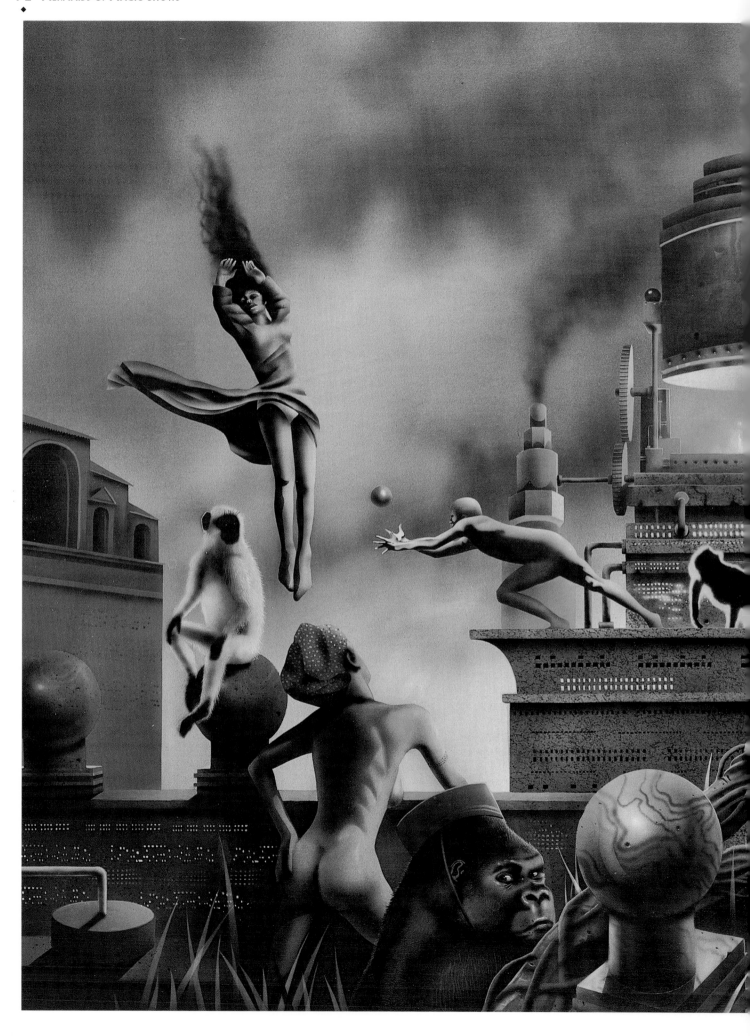

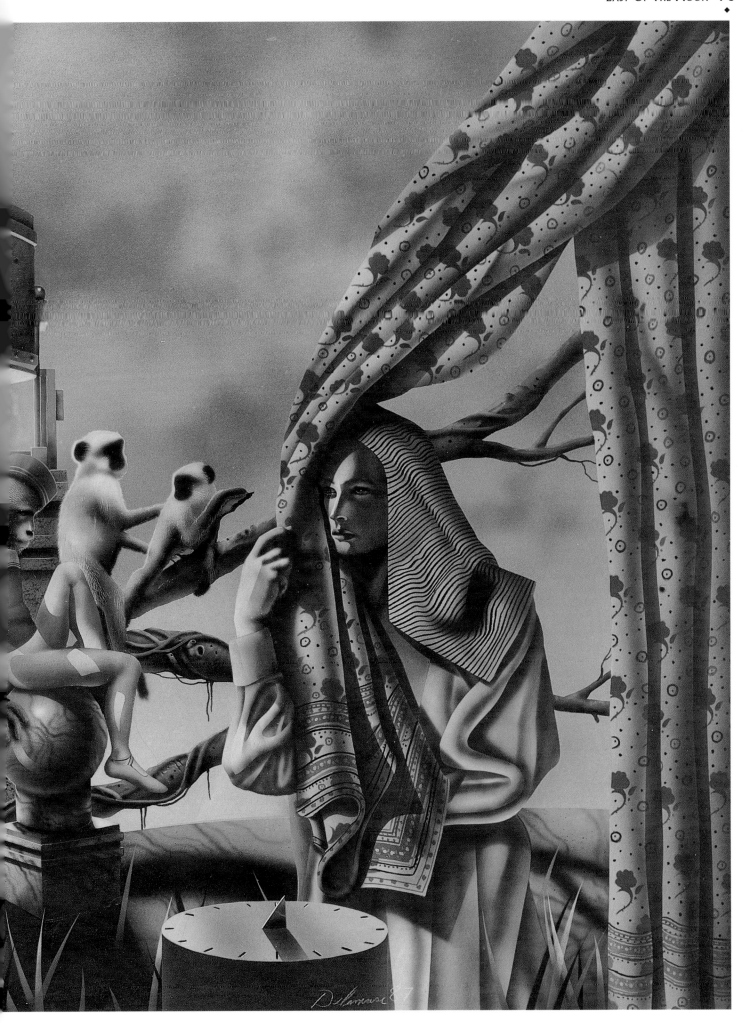

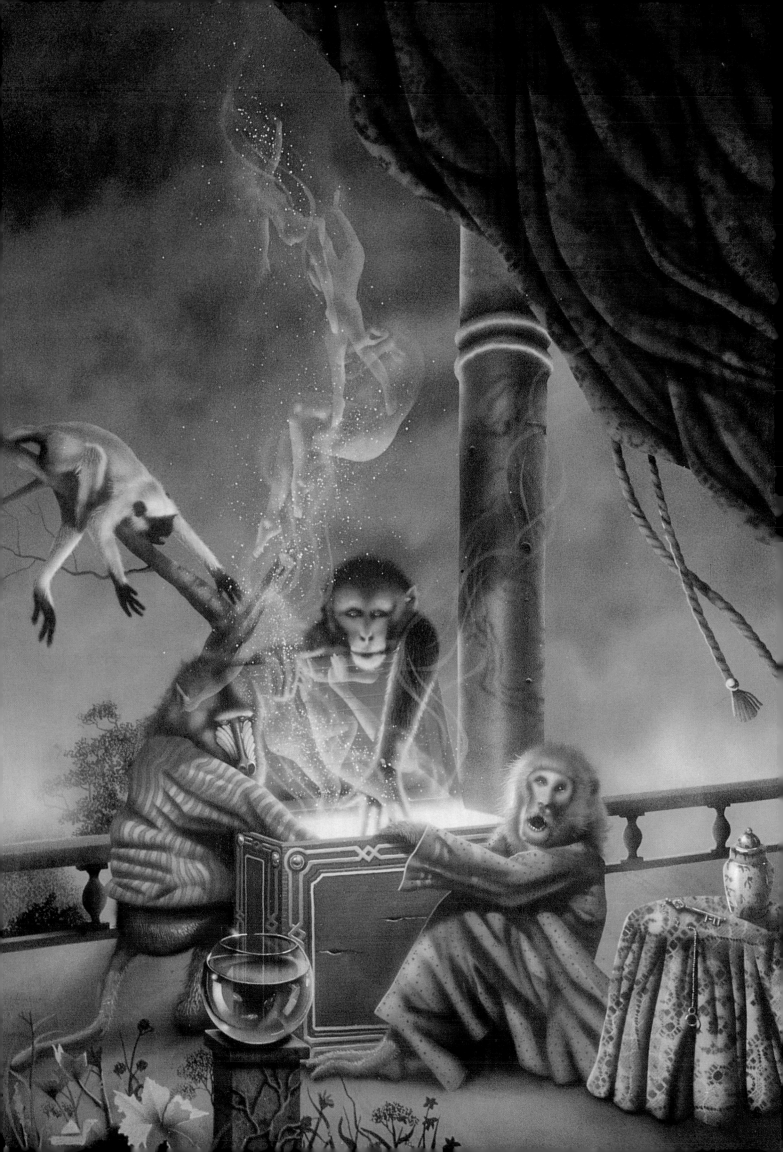

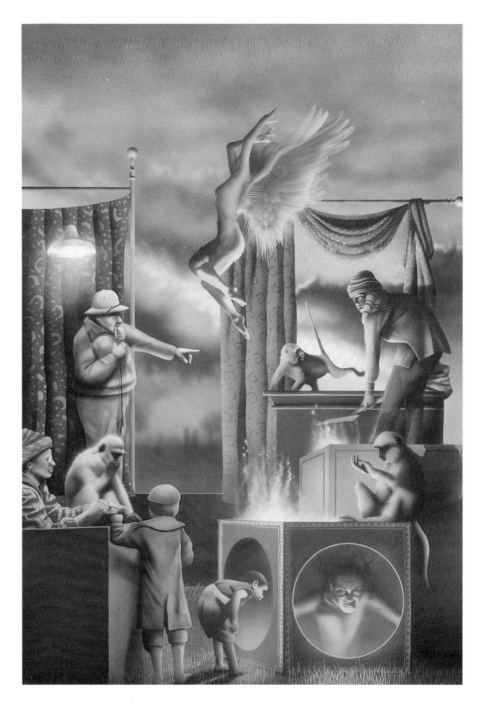

◁ **PANDORA'S BOX** 1988

Gouache 18 x 24in (45 x 60cm)

A reworking of a favourite theme, the scenario being that this is maybe the second generation since the box has been resealed, when these monkeys come along and open it.

△ **CRADLE OF PALE FIRE** 1990

Gouache 20 x 26in (50 x 65cm)

Although the theme of travelling circus shows is a favourite one, Delamare, in fact, hates modern circuses. This composition reminds him of the travelling shows of moving images in the seventeenth century, which astonished and delighted audiences. 'It's hard to be wowed by anything so simple these days,' Delamare comments rather wistfully.

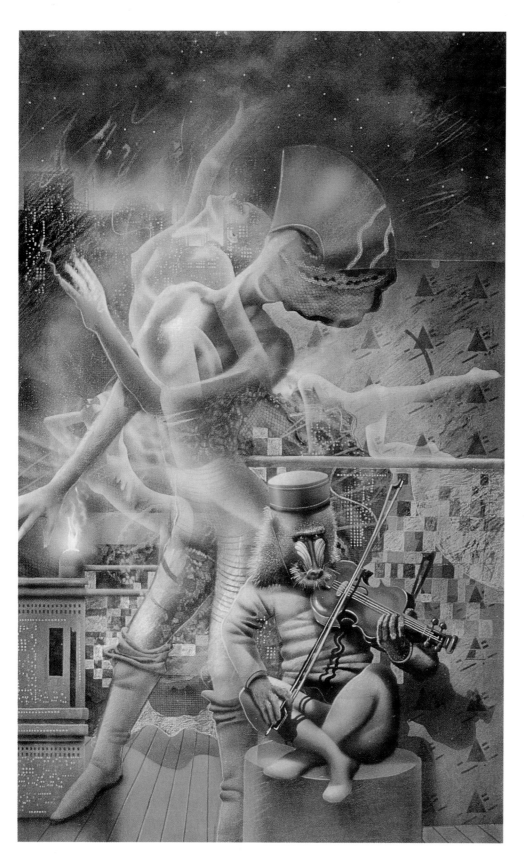

◁ **EMPIRE** 1987

Mixed media 18 x 26in (45 x 65cm)

The starting point for this painting was thinking about Rome burning while Nero fiddled. The experiment here was mixing different textural qualities, or degrees of realism.

▷ **THE INFREQUENT BRIDE** 1988

Gouache 20 x 26in (50 x 65cm)

A faint echo here of Marcel Duchamp's the 'Nude Descending the Staircase'. The ghostly figures in Delamare's pictures are not ghosts as such, but metaphors for how tricky it is keeping a constant and consistent image in the mind of someone you feel close to.

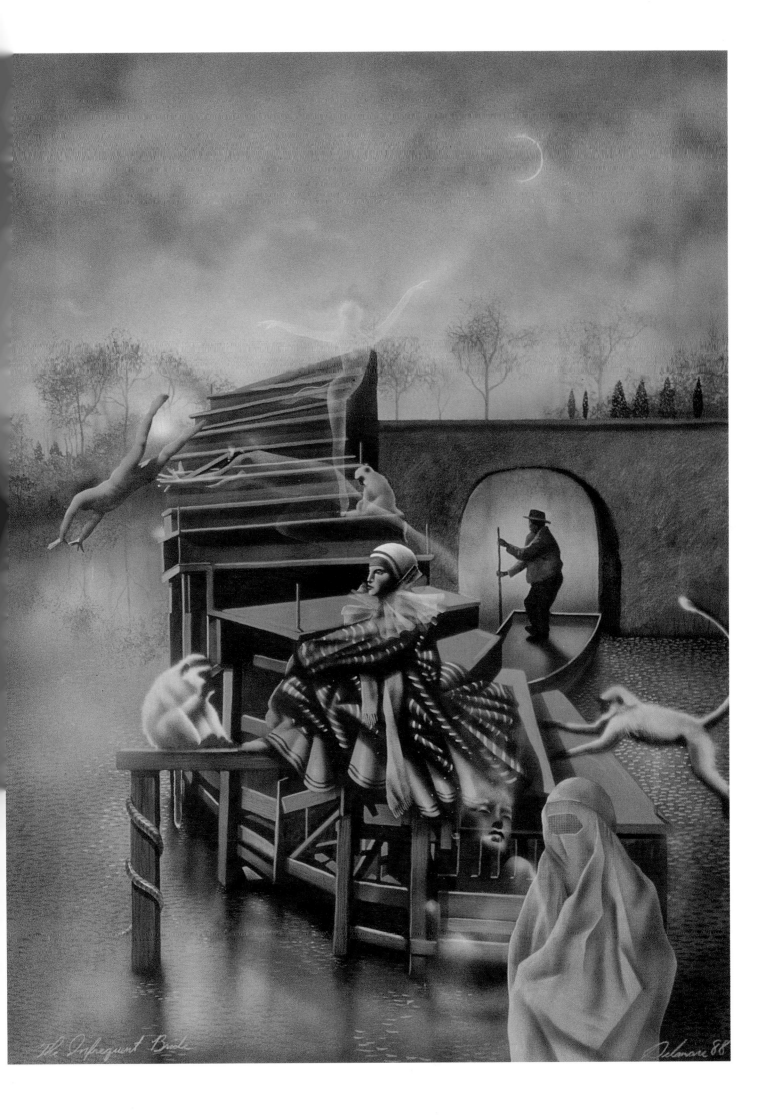

The Infrequent Bride   Delmare 88

BOOK ILLUSTRATION

I f a single picture is like looking through the window of a mysterious house, then an illustrated book is like opening the door and exploring within. That, for Delamare, is the appeal of storytelling.

The first children's book he was invited to illustrate was *The Hawk's Tale* by John Balaban published by Harcourt Brace in 1988. The story had a strong *Wind in the Willows* feeling to it, and Delamare was very happy with the illustrations he produced for it. The job, however, did demand some very rapid learning on how to tackle a publishing commission. He also had some uncomfortable surprises along the way, such as the publisher halving the size of the book and thus losing or diminishing details of the pictures designed for the larger format.

Without preparation he was also introduced to the practice of 'peeling' or 'stripping' pictures for use with the cylindrical scanners often used for making illustration plates. This means that when a picture is presented on the usual stiff illustration board, the surface layer is peeled off so it can be wrapped around the cylinder. Having had no idea this might happen, Delamare was at first horrified. 'What does that involve? Do you have experts to do it?' he asked. 'Well, we'd rather have you do it,' they replied, 'because we'd feel bad about it if the artwork got torn.' Delamare did do it himself, which was very scary at first, but by the end he was stripping the top layer off his treasured paintings as if it was the most natural thing in the world.

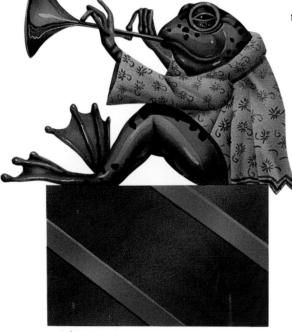

END PAPER I 1992
Acrylic 10 x 10in (25 x 25cm)
Illustration for *The Twelve Days of Christmas*, Unicorn Books.

His next children's book was *The Steadfast Tin Soldier* published in 1989 by Unicorn Books. The connection with Unicorn came about, curiously, because they had rejected Delamare's earlier project, *Creature Comforts* – a selection of anthropomorphic pictures accompanied by rhymes – but liked the artwork enough to want more.

An unforeseen side effect of the *Tin Soldier* commission was the ending of Delamare's relationship with his then girlfriend. Stuck for a model for the rat on the front cover, he asked her to pose. This might have been all right had it been kept secret, but word got out and as a standing joke it turned into the proverbial camel's last straw. That's his theory anyway. They have since been reconciled as good friends.

Also published in 1989 was *The Nutcracker*, the next project for Unicorn, some samples of which are shown in this chapter. To get interesting angles on some of the key features, Delamare made models of them, a practice he has continued to some extent with every book since.

His third project with Unicorn was *The Twelve Days of Christmas*, which had an intriguing format. The idea was for the picture to follow the words of the carol, but after every three plates to have a full double-page spread of a scene incorporating all the characters introduced thus far, till by the end it looks like something painted by Bosch or Bruegel.

While it was very gratifying to be thus suddenly in demand as an illustrator of traditional or other people's texts, what Delamare really wanted was to illustrate his own. Furthermore, he wanted to do something over which he had complete artistic control. This is how *The Christmas Secret* came about, something he felt very strongly compelled to do and which he was determined to finish on his own terms regardless of what anyone else thought of it afterwards.

The seed of the story was a piece from *Creature Comforts* showing a lion dressed as Santa Claus. From this everything else developed in a very 'organic' way: 'There was definitely no linear progression. I just worked away at bits and pieces of it till the project looked finished.' Apart from anything else, being in control of the text meant he could ensure that the words and pictures were fully complementary instead of overlapping or cramping each other, which had sometimes happened before. At times he felt really spoiled, it felt so much like the perfect way to work.

The story tells of a gentle old lion called Richardson and a tiny but brave mouse who together make Christmas Day possible for their village. The text was fine-tuned by a friend, Pearl Watkins, when it

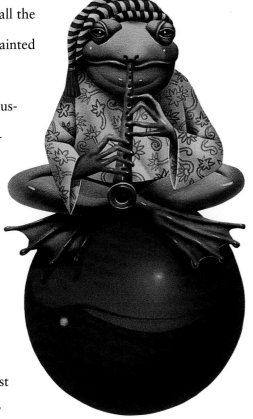

END PAPER II 1992
Acrylic 10 x 10in (25 x 25cm)
Illustration for *The Twelve Days of Christmas*, Unicorn Books.

reached the point that Delamare could no longer be objective about it. As he knew the character so well, Delamare posed for the lion himself and worked from photographs taken by a friend.

So far so perfect, but it began to seem that maybe it had all been too good to be true when it came to getting the work published. Rejection after rejection came in depressingly quick succession. Then Delamare was introduced by a friend to Cooper Edens, an artist and writer who had enjoyed considerable success in the United States with picture books. Edens loved *The Christmas* Secret and suggested an approach to Green Tiger in California, a small but highly esteemed publisher of picture books. The suggestion turned out to be a stroke of double luck because not only did Green Tiger accept the book, but they were taken over by Simon and Schuster while it was in the course of preparation, so its possible distribution immediately increased tenfold.

THE KIDNAPPING 1988
Gouache 16 x 20in (40 x 50cm)
Unpublished illustration for *The Christmas Secret*, Simon and Schuster. This picture followed a tangent of the story, which was eventually dropped because the plot was becoming too tangled and long.

Although it was only indirectly their baby, Simon and Schuster were enthusiastic about the book and proved extremely sympathetic to work with. The only area of disagreement concerned colouring. Delamare's original pictures were in sepia tints which the publishers felt were too colourless, especially since printing sepia pictures is still a four-colour process. As a compromise, Delamare decided to treat the pictures as tinted photographs, laying washes of acrylic ink over some areas. 'I approached the retouching with trepidation because I hate retouching finished work, but the result was satisfying all round.'

This was his first use of acrylics, a medium he now uses almost totally because of the luminous effect of light reflecting through the transparent ink from the surface below.

When *The Christmas Secret* was published in 1991 it was

warmly received, so the question arose of what to do next. Delamare made a few suggestions, which fell on stony ground, then out of the blue the publishers came back with the suggestion of doing *Cinderella*. At first the artist was reluctant. When he tried the idea out in his mind, the only response was a set of memory flashes from the Walt Disney version, with which there seemed no point in competing. But he was being offered carte blanche with the pictures and the chance to rewrite the story in his own way. Further mining for inspiration struck gold – if he set the story in Venice all preconceptions would be swept away.

MR PINDAR THE LAMPLIGHTER 1988
Gouache 20 x 20in (50 x 50cm)
Unpublished embellishment for *The Christmas Secret*, Simon and Schuster. This illustration did in fact connect with the main story but for unknown reasons was not used.

The next problem was finding a suitable model for Cinders. On beginning work he had a fairly specific idea of how she should look but knew noone who fitted the bill. Then one day – joy! While out with his girlfriend Maryanne there came walking down the street towards them the perfect person. Maryannne happened to be aquainted with the lady, with the wonderful name, Asia, who was both willing to pose, and proved to be a tremendous catalyst for the project as a whole, having a different-world quality that served to inspire much of the imagery in the book. Delamare remembers: 'I have never had such an effortless time painting someone. She almost painted herself, which is a good indicator of being on the right track. If you have to fight something there is probably something wrong with it.'

The Christmas Secret and *Cinderella* are Delamare's ideal way of working in books, being given the maximum of artistic freedom and in addition, control over the text, which for him is always subordinate to the pictures.

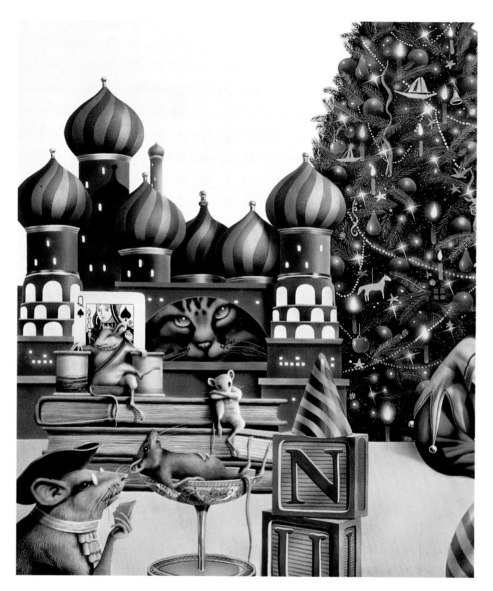

△ **ONION DOME CASTLE** 1989
Acrylic 20 x 26in (50 x 65cm)
Back cover for *The Nutcracker*,
Unicorn Books.

▷ **OWL CLOCK** 1989
Acrylic 20 x 26in (50 x 65cm)
Illustration for *The Nutcracker*, Unicorn
Books.

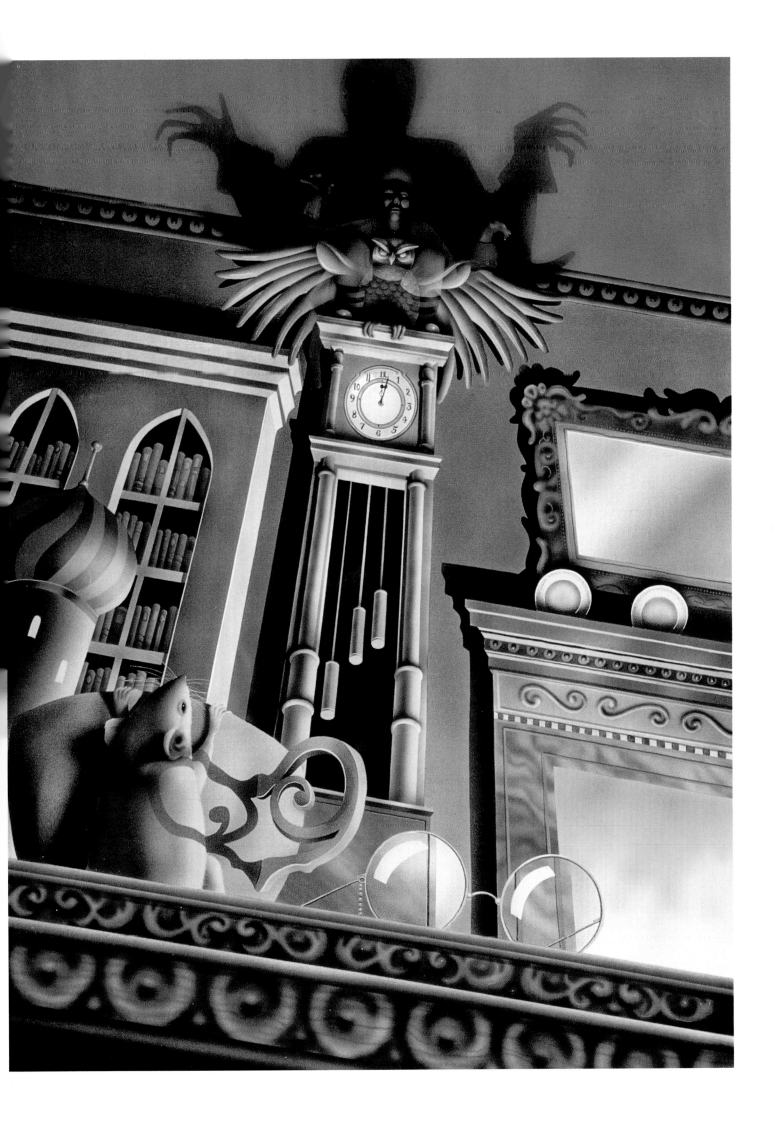

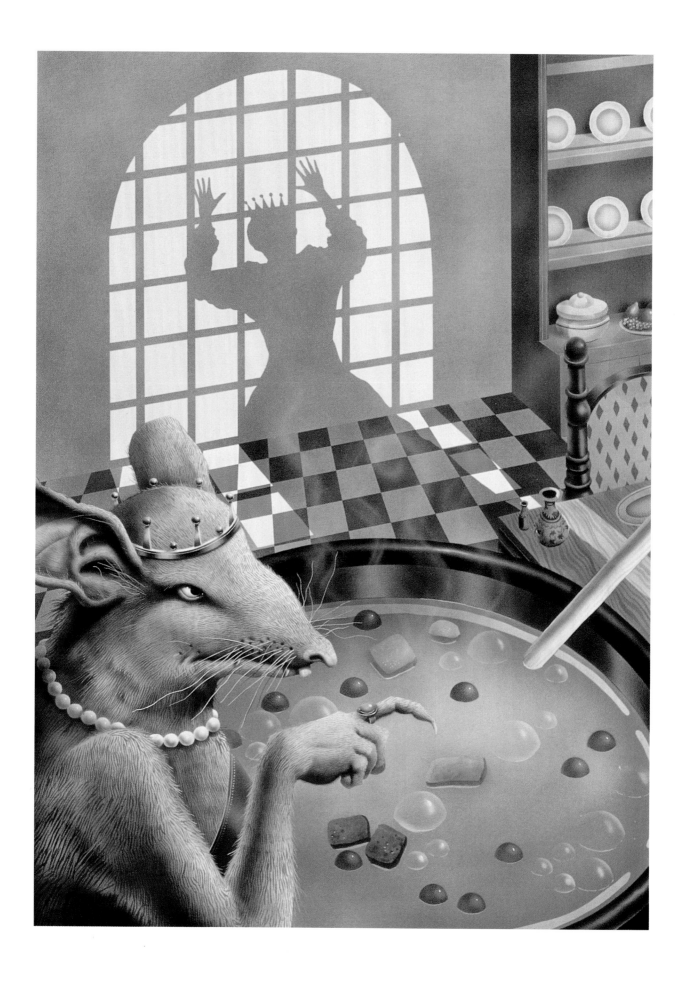

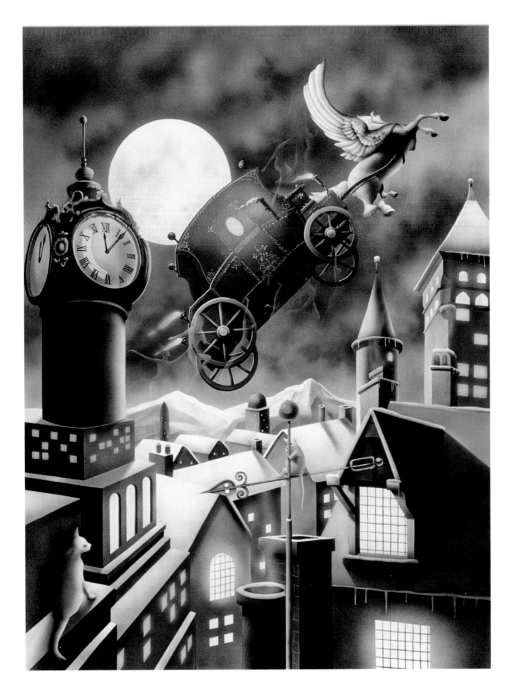

◁ **DAME MOUSERINK** 1989
Acrylic 20 x 26in (50 x 65cm)
Illustration for *The Nutcracker*, Unicorn
Books.

△ **THE GOLDEN COACH** 1989
Acrylic 20 x 26in (50 x 65cm)
Illustration for *The Nutcracker*, Unicorn
Books.

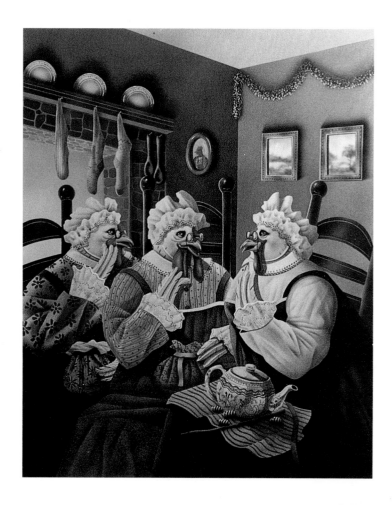

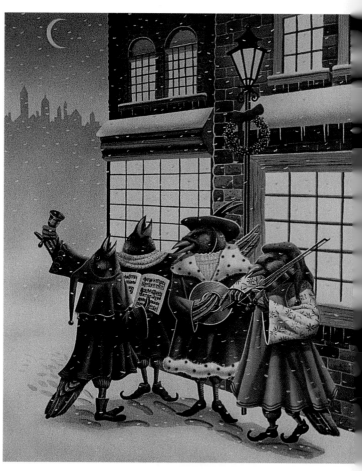

△ **THREE FRENCH HENS** 1992
Acrylic 20 x 26in (50 x 65cm)
Illustration for *The Twelve Days of Christmas*, Unicorn Books.

◁ **FOUR CALLING BIRDS** 1992
Acrylic 20 x 26in (50 x 65cm)
Illustration for *The Twelve Days of Christmas*, Unicorn Books.

▷ **SIX GEESE** 1992
Acrylic 20 x 26in (50 x 65cm)
Illustration for *The Twelve Days of Christmas*, Unicorn Books.

▷ ▷ **NINE LADIES DANCING** 1992
Acrylic 20 x 26in (50 x 65cm)
Illustration for *The Twelve Days of Christmas*, Unicorn Books.

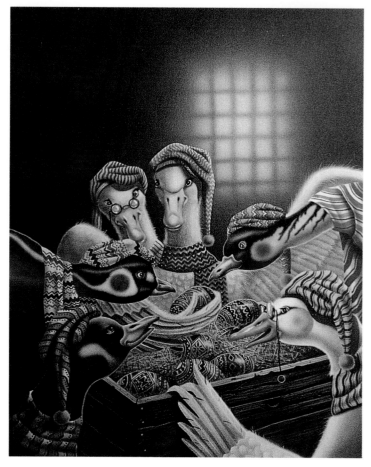

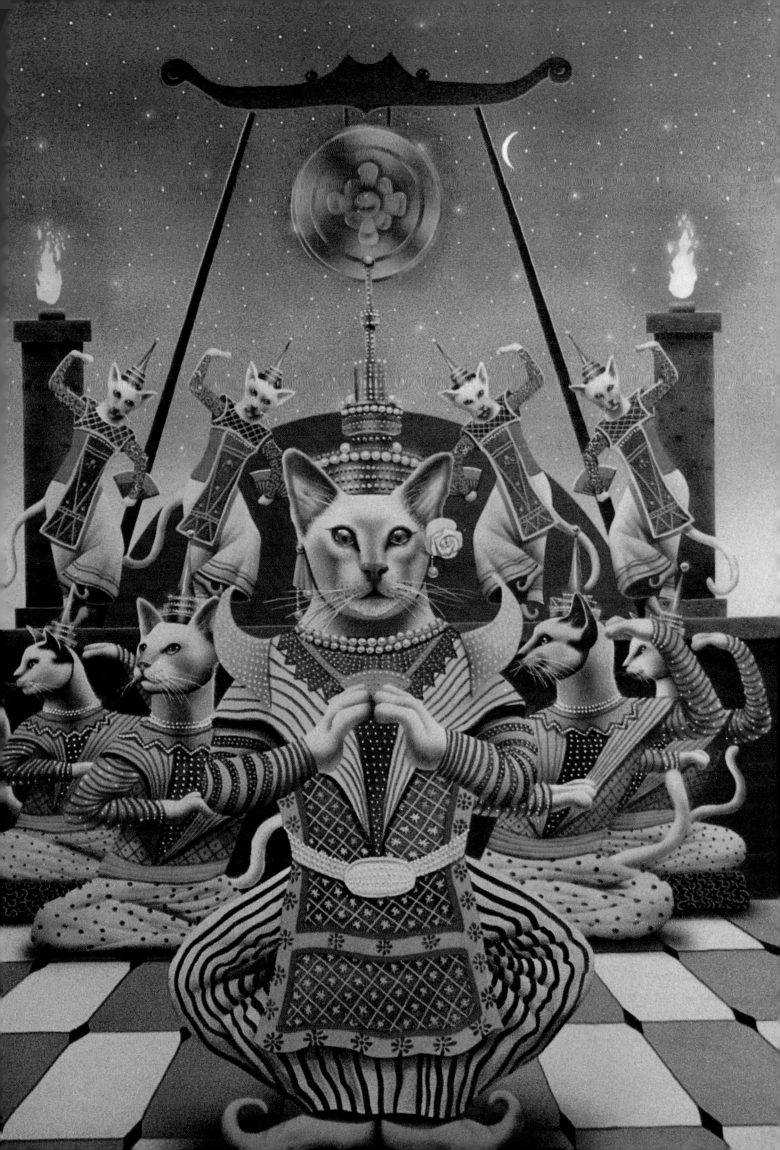

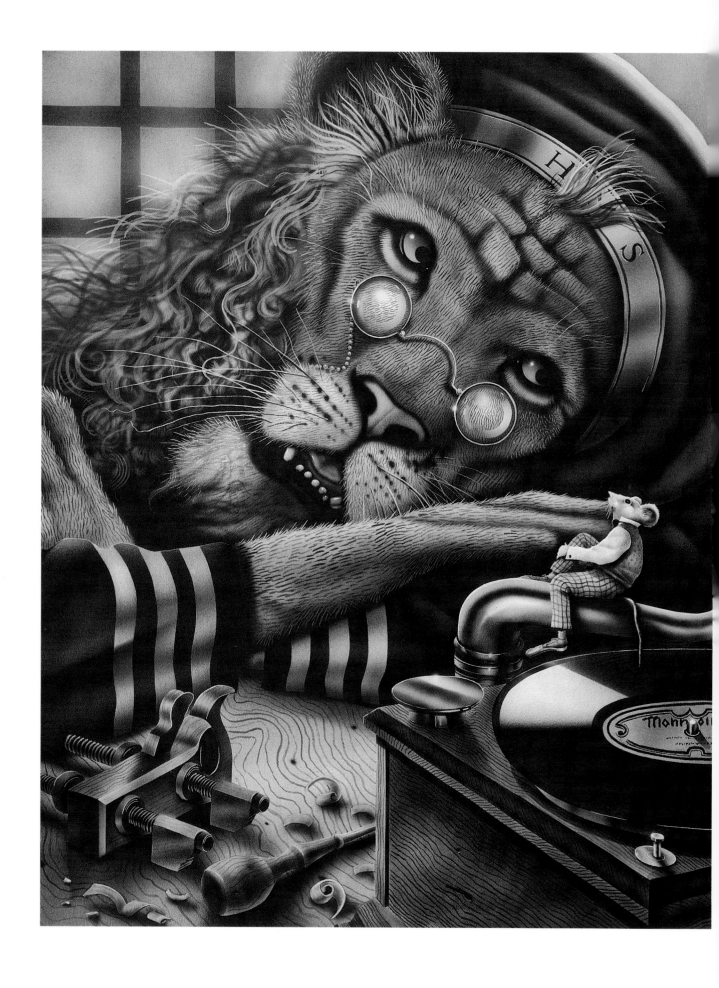

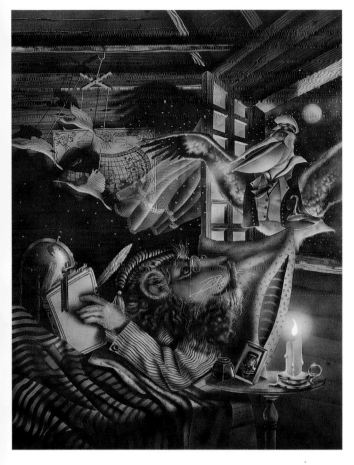

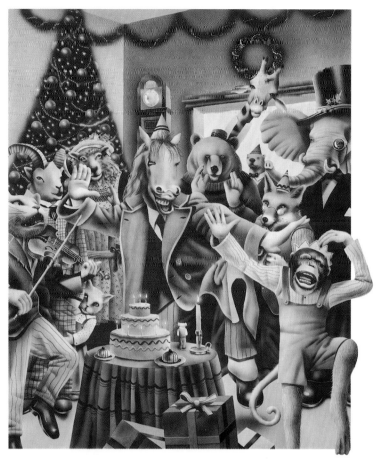

◁ **RICHARDSON AND TAG** 1988
Gouache and acrylic 11 x 16in (27 x 40cm)
Illustration for *The Christmas Secret*, Simon
and Schuster.

△ **RICHARDSON SURPRISED BY QUILTY**
1988
Gouache and acrylic 11 x 16in (27 x 40cm)
Illustration for *The Christmas Secret*, Simon
and Schuster.

◁ **THE CHRISTMAS PARTY** 1988
Gouache and acrylic 11 x 16in (27 x 40cm)
Illustration for The Christmas Secret, Simon
and Schuster.

▷ **TAG AND THE LETTER** 1988
Gouache and acrylic 11 x 16in (27 x 40cm)
Illustration for *The Christmas Secret*, Simon
and Schuster.

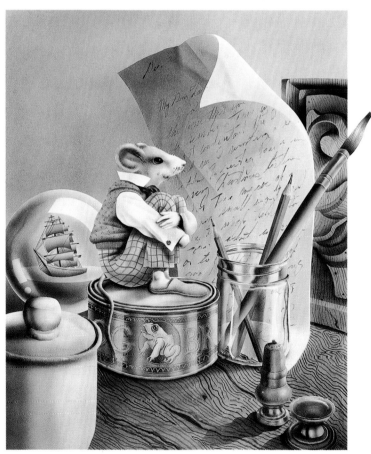

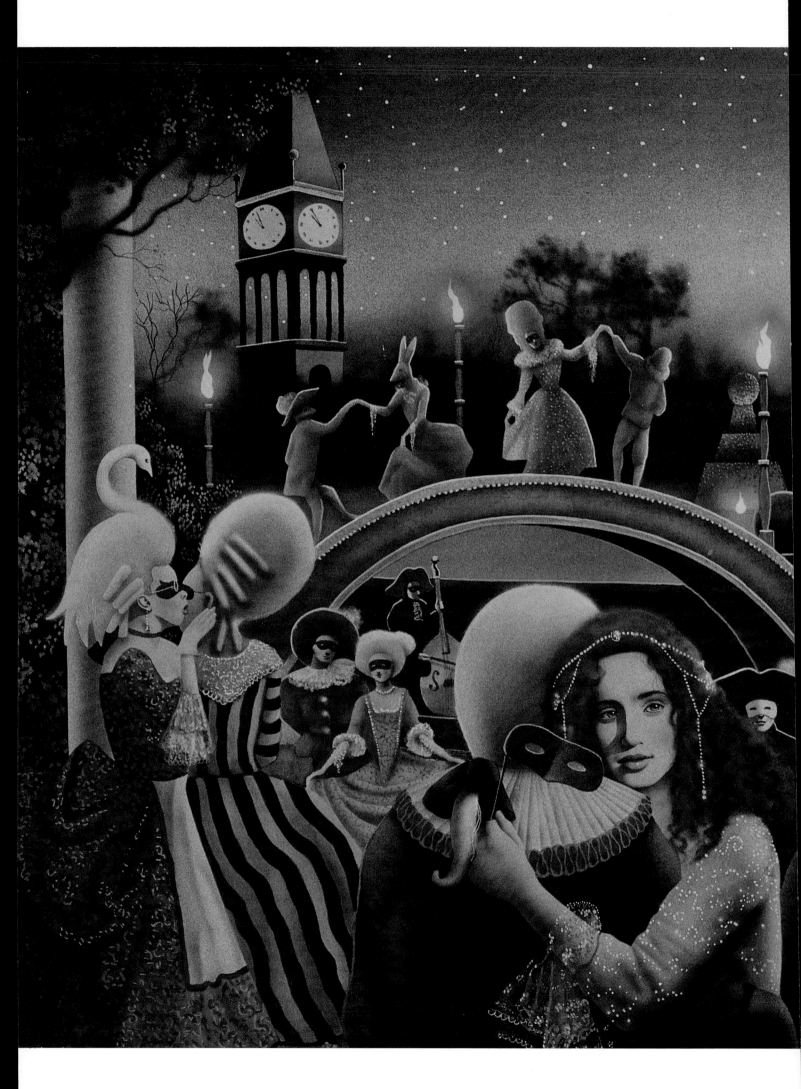

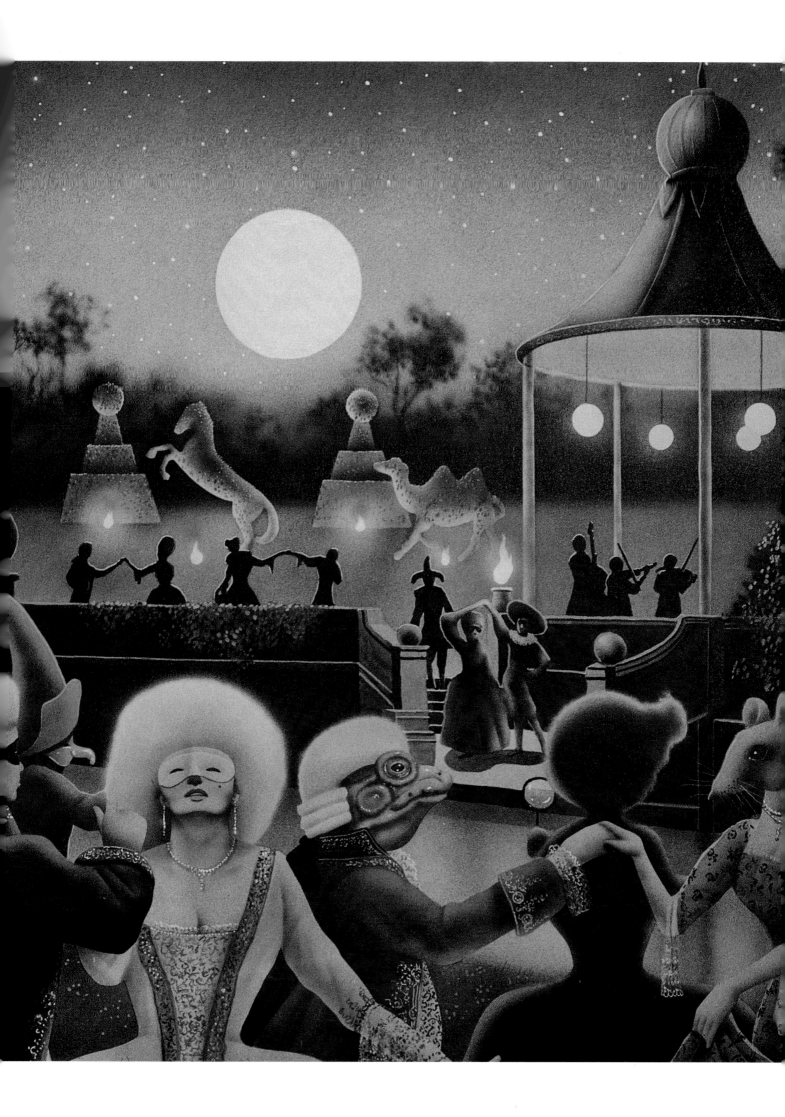

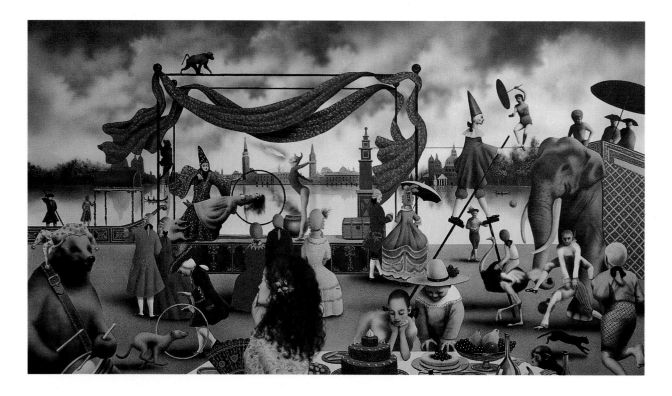

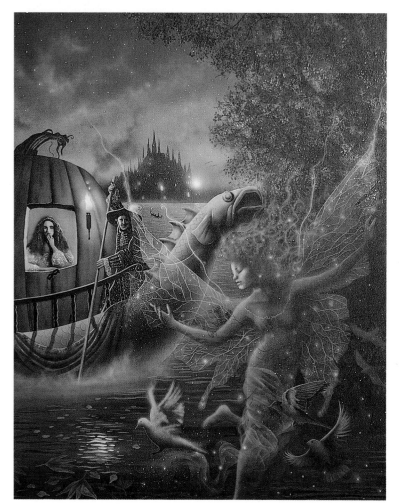

◁ ◁ **THE MASKED BALL** 1993
Acrylic 16 x 24in (40 x 60cm)
Illustration for *Cinderella*, Simon and
Schuster.

△ **CINDERELLA'S BIRTHDAY** 1993
Acrylic 16 x 24in (40 x 60cm)
Illustration for *Cinderella*, Simon and
Schuster.

◁ **FAIRY MOTHER CREATES THE
GONDOLA** 1993
Acrylic 11 x 16in (27 x 40cm)
Illustration for *Cinderella* Simon and
Schuster.

▷ **CINDERELLA AWAITING HER
FATHER'S SHIP** 1993
Acrylic 11 x 16in (27 x 40cm)
Illustration for *Cinderella*, Simon and
Schuster.

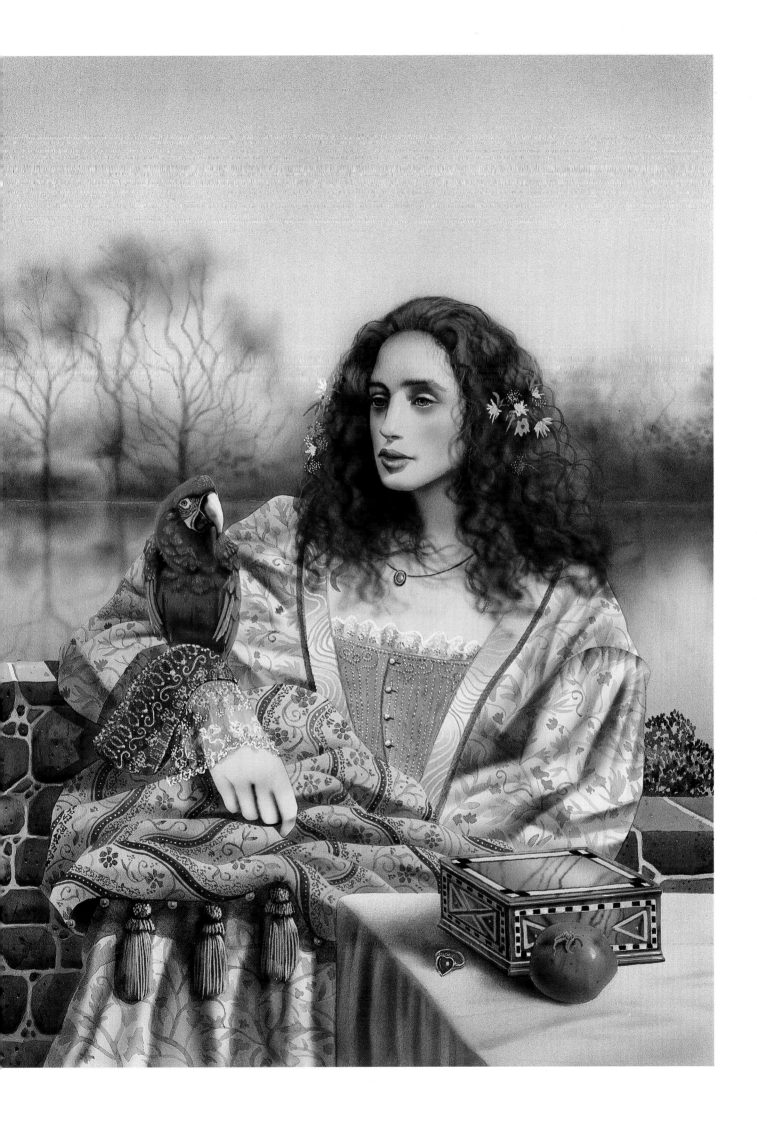

THE MASK & WIG CLUB

GALLERY SHOWINGS

In his career as an artist David Delamare is very aware of the decisive part luck has played. Being in the right place at the right time is, he deems, as necessary as innate talent or hard work. Although he has long had a clear idea of where he would like to be as an artist, he has not been following any fixed plan for getting there. Just as his compositions are rarely calculated in advance but just spiral outwards from some germ of an idea or observation on the wings of intuition, so has his career. The seed of his career was simply the urge to make a living as an artist. Achieving that end has been a combination of following his instincts and serendipity, a word that drops frequently into his conversation.

Galleries were a far from obvious route at the outset because, particularly in the United States, they tend to avoid figurative and narrative paintings. Delamare attributes this to a preference for home-grown art forms, such as abstract expressionism, just as musicians tend to favour jazz. He has noticed that European galleries favour narrative pictures much more because, presumably, that is what all European art is rooted in.

Galleries, however, particularly the Graystone gallery just down the road from his studio, were to prove his liberation from the commercial graphic work which was his mainstay for a while after leaving college. One day, while chatting with the owners of the Graystone Gallery, it emerged that he was an artist, and they suggested that he bring in some pictures.

He had recently started the series of anthropomorphic pictures, which figure largely in this book, so he took in a batch of sixteen, which immediately delighted the owners. They had had a show cancelled by an artist the previous week, so they offered the available space to Delamare. It was his road to Damascus, the show was a sell-out and launched him as an independent artist. Graystone has remained his main gallery outlet ever since, though his work has also spread to others along the West Coast down into California and up into Washington State.

Touting his own work is not something that comes easily to Delamare and fortunately he has not often been forced into it. Generally, people call him after seeing his work somewhere – the snowball effect. Publishing is a great help because it raises his profile, and magazine interviews are particularly effective. Sometimes, years after an article is published, he gets a call from some private collection asking if a particular picture featured in the magazine is for sale.

The style of work featured in this chapter is one he has developed with specifically galleries in mind. This work is, he feels, more 'organic' than his narrative pictures, in that the painting develops quite spontaneously instead of being assembled rather like a jigsaw, as is necessary with his more detailed work. This style began as one of the deliberate periodic experiments with which Delamare staves off his fear of stagnation, and just happened to prove acceptable. This looser, more abstract style is a refreshing antidote to the lengthy periods of concentration needed on a set of book illustrations, for example. The different approaches rejuvenate each other and help keep both from losing their edge.

HIS MASTER'S VOICE 1983
Mixed media 14 x 20in (35 x 50cm)
An important departure piece, which marks the beginning of Delamare's looser 'organic' style.

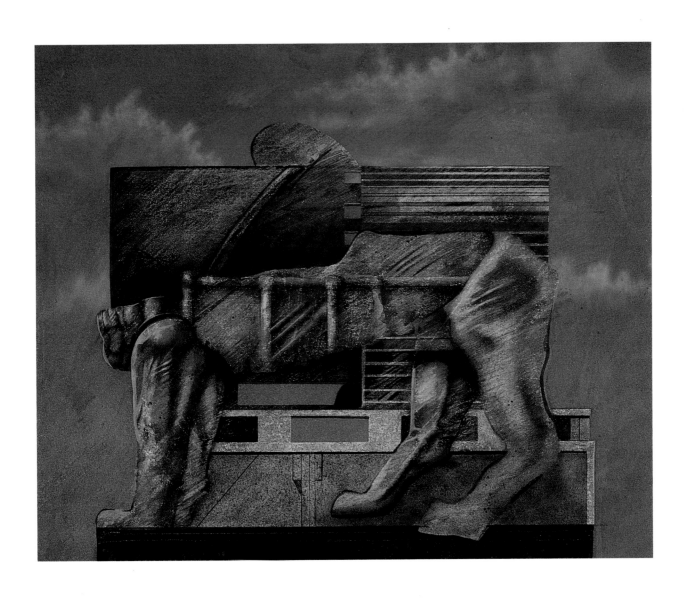

At college Delamare studied both graphics and fine art and found that the work he really liked doing tended to 'fall into the cracks between the two'. It still tends to confound definition. Most of the pieces in this book have the feeling of illustrations but do not refer to any text and have not been produced on commission. It looks like graphic work but is produced in a fine-art manner, in that he paints whatever he feels needs to be painted and then offers it for sale. Fortunately, it seems to make no difference. Whatever prejudice there is in the fine-art world against figurative work – and in some quarters it is considerable – it has had little impact on David Delamare. Galleries exhibit all aspects of his work, and it brightens the lives of their customers enough to allow him to pursue his own imaginative course and pay the bills, which is a rare enough achievement for any artist, let alone one who quietly flouts all conventions.

What directions his work may take in the future it is hard to say because Delamare himself never knows when a passing idea might turn into a fresh departure. What is fairly certain is that he will continue to spring surprises on his public because a willingness to experiment is built into his relationship with the imagination, along with the humility to recognize or accept when the result is a disaster. Add to this undiminished curiosity, a sense of wonder about life, large measures of talent and originality and you have a recipe for much more work of the same quality to come.

Although he commented earlier on the 'anxiety' that comes with being professionally dependent on a faculty such as the imagination, which cannot be conjured up at will, he nevertheless has a wide range of techniques for keeping his mind open to the promptings of inspiration when they do come. For instance, he loves browsing randomly in a local shop, which claims to stock all the magazines published in the US, never knowing when something will trigger his unconscious.

There is also a 'psychological environment game' he sometimes plays when he has the germ of an idea. From the same starting point he proceeds to paint with different music playing in the background – Mozart one day, Wagner the next – and generally the idea takes off in totally different directions. 'The question with creative states is that you never really know what affects them. You can never tell how everything in your environment feeds into the subconscious.'

How the imagination works remains a mystery, but what is possible is to keep the unconscious well (if randomly) fed and pay attention when it speaks. This is what David Delamare does – exquisitely.

▷ **ANOTHER BLUE WORLD** 1988
Acrylic 16 x 22in (40 x 55cm)
For Delamare the nude is the perfect form, containing all the elements of aesthetics. If, on his deathbed, he is offered a choice between seeing, for example the Grand Canyon or a nude, geology will stand no chance. Here the smooth forms of the body are accentuated by the frenetic activity in the background.

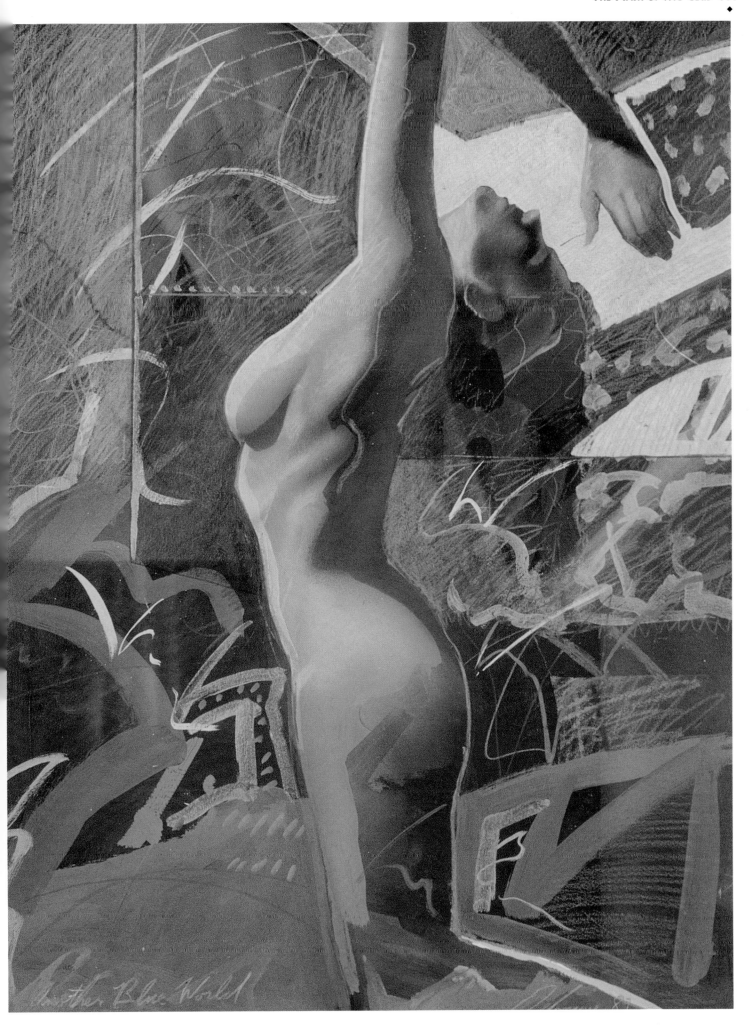

POUR DOWN LIKE SILVER 1989
*Gouache, pencil and pastel 18 x
28in (45 x 70cm)*

A spontaneous drawing derived from a
model going through various dance
poses. The picture was bought by a
visiting English aunt as a rather bold
present for her husband. She assumed
that even if he did approve of it, he
would tuck it away somewhere out of
visitors' sight. Not only did he
approve, he loved it, and hung it in
pride of place in the living room. 'You
never know what people will be
attracted to,' Delamare says. 'It never
ceases to amaze me.'

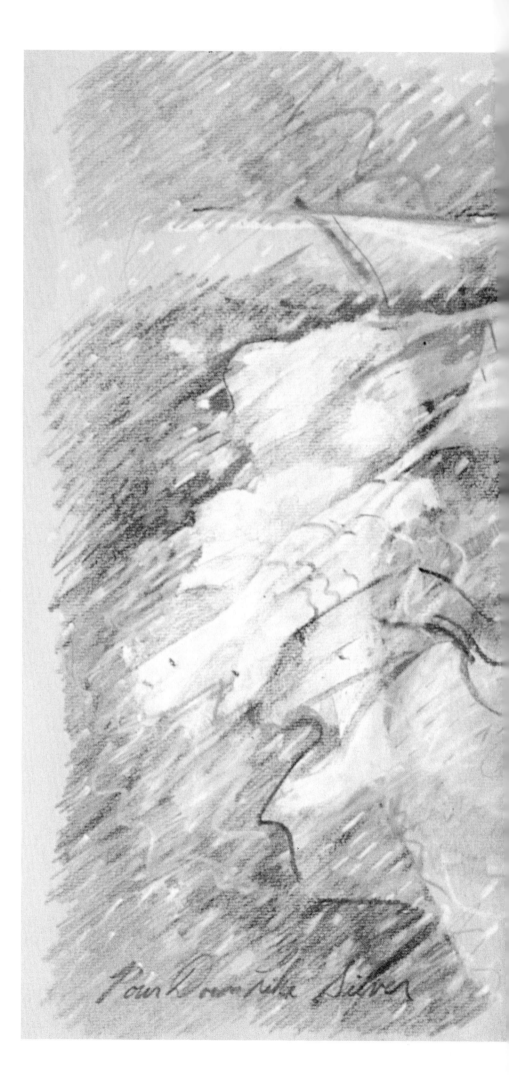

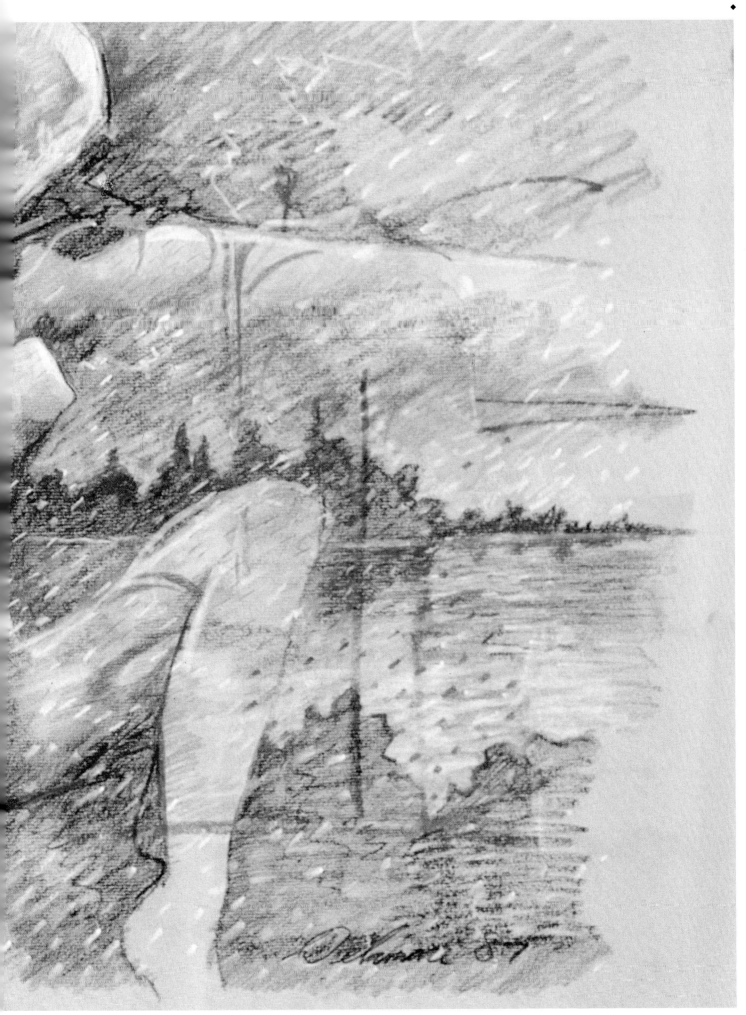

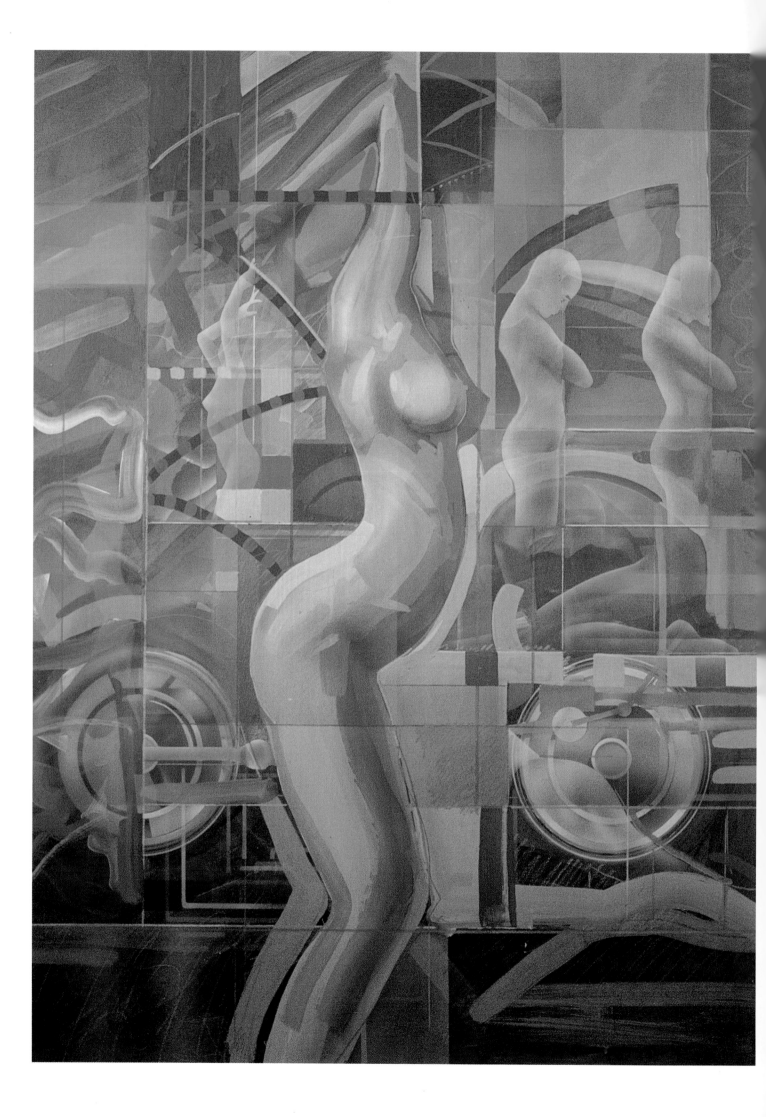

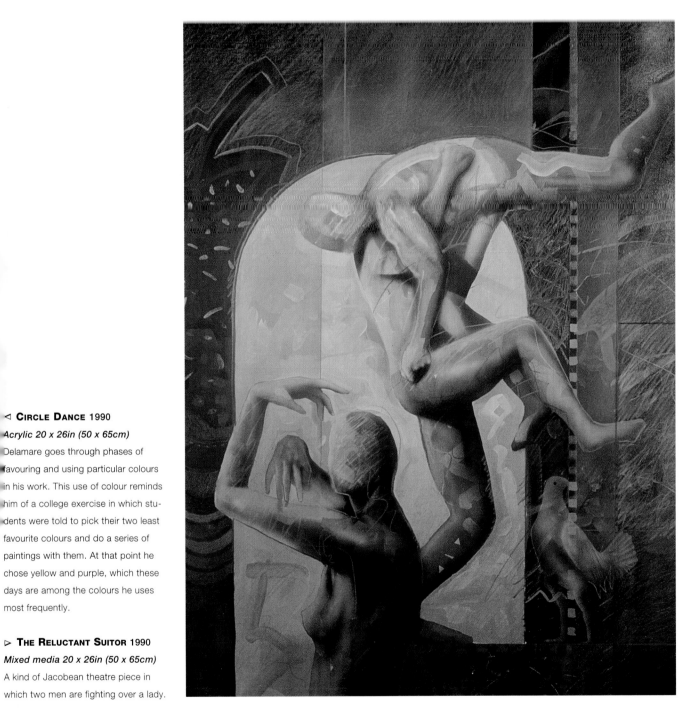

◁ **CIRCLE DANCE** 1990
Acrylic 20 x 26in (50 x 65cm)
Delamare goes through phases of
favouring and using particular colours
in his work. This use of colour reminds
him of a college exercise in which students were told to pick their two least
favourite colours and do a series of
paintings with them. At that point he
chose yellow and purple, which these
days are among the colours he uses
most frequently.

▷ **THE RELUCTANT SUITOR** 1990
Mixed media 20 x 26in (50 x 65cm)
A kind of Jacobean theatre piece in
which two men are fighting over a lady.

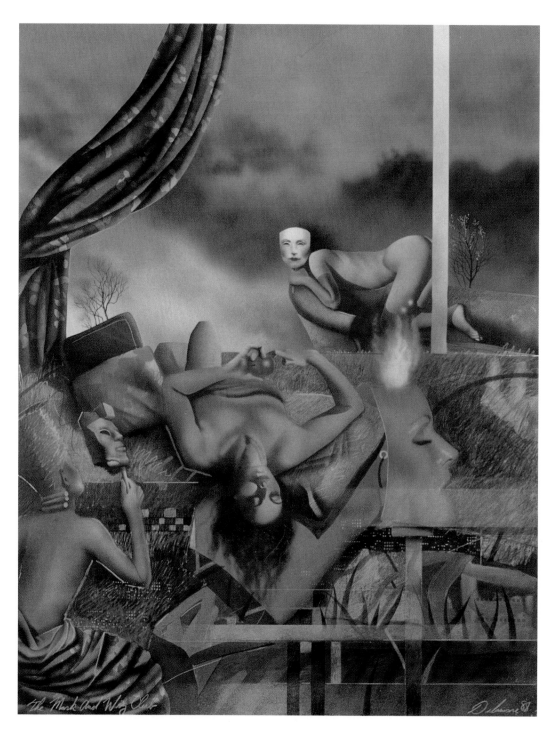

△ **THE MASK AND WIG CLUB** 1988
Mixed media 20 x 26in (50 x 65cm)
Someone commented that women
might find this bordello stage show
piece sexist. Delamare riposted that he
has always tried to portray his nudes
with integrity. At this point an attractive
woman came in and bought the painting for herself, not her husband, which
seemed the best possible validation.

▷ **BECKETT** 1990
Acrylic 20 x 26in (50 x 65cm)
Illustration for an article in the Portland
arts magazine *The Rose* to mark the
death of one of Delamare's favourite
playwrights. The picture is a compila-
tion of scenes from different plays.

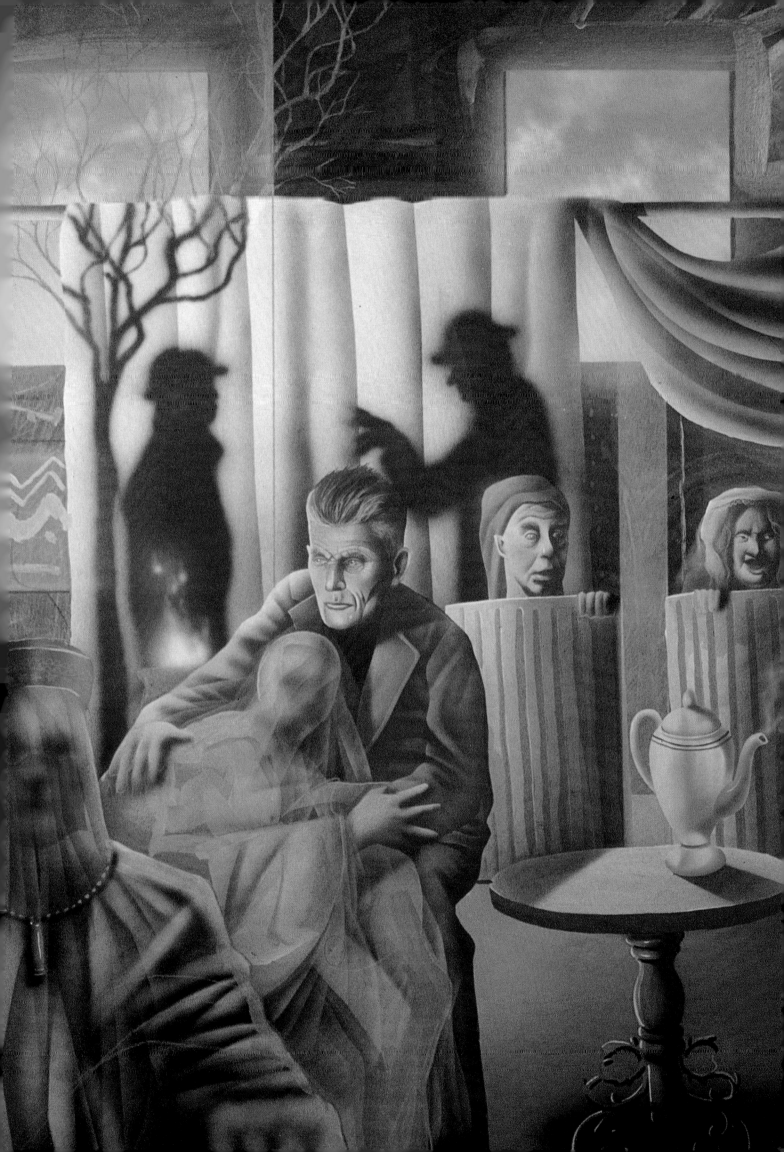

▷ **DOG AND LADDER** 1990
Mixed media 18 x 18in (45 x 45cm)
The influence of photography shows in
the layering of images against the grid-
like background. Some areas are
heavily textured with oil sticks to contrast with the smooth airbrushing.

▷ ▷ **THE GOLDEN MEAN** 1990
Mixed media 20 x 26in (50 x 65cm)
This may prove a new departure point
– mingling two- and three-dimensional
imagery with areas of ambivalence
where one is not sure which is which.

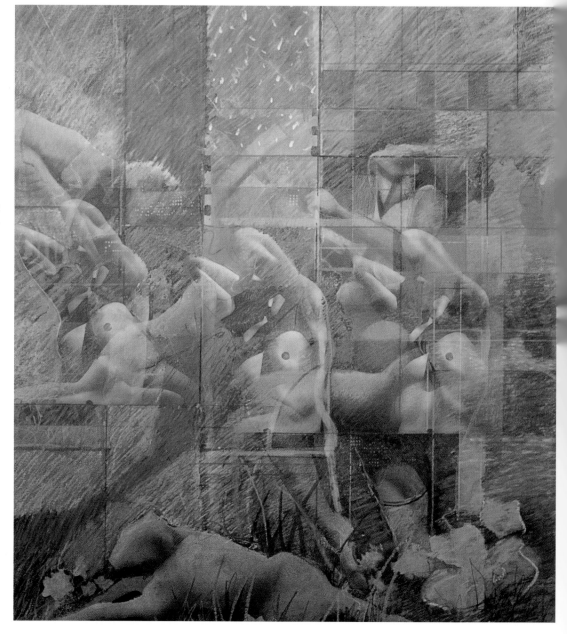

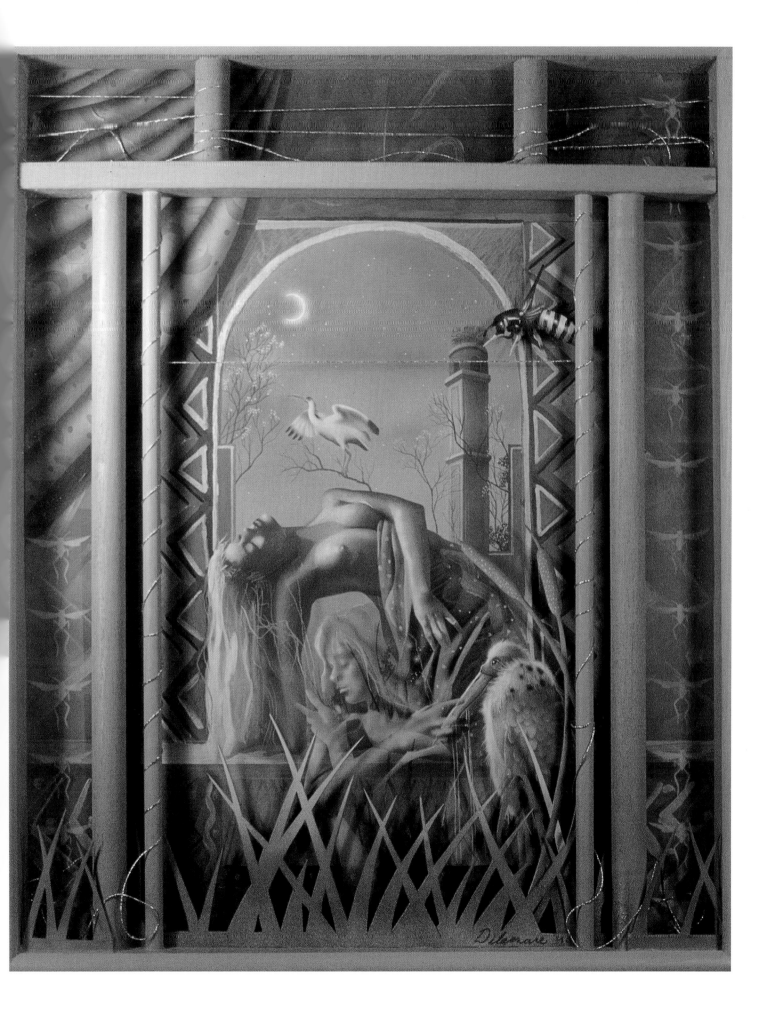

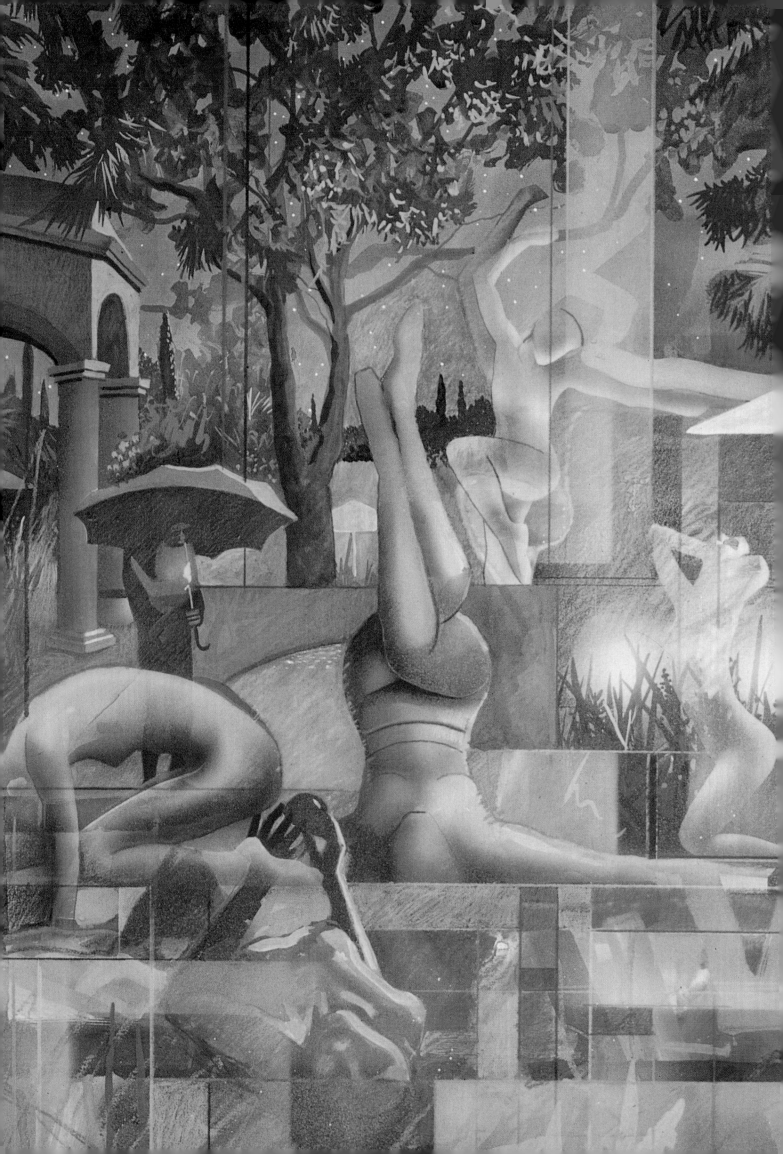

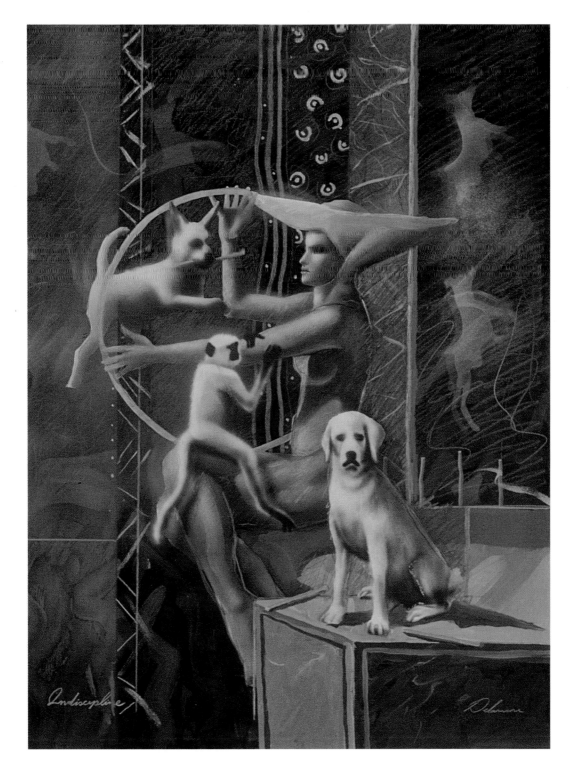

◁ **THE GREEN APPLE** 1985

Gouache 20 x 26in (50 x 65cm)

This painting was inspired by an intriguing magazine picture of a naked Australian Aborigine lighting a cigar while sheltering under an umbrella in a rainstorm.

△ **INDISCIPLINE** 1990

Gouache 20 x 26in (50 x 65cm)

Often, when composing pictures, Delamare visualizes the figures as silhouettes. In this case this led him to add the curious headdress to add interest to the profile. When repeating images he often cuts templates. The dog motif in the background is the result of this practice. The title refers to the recalcitrant mutt in the foreground.

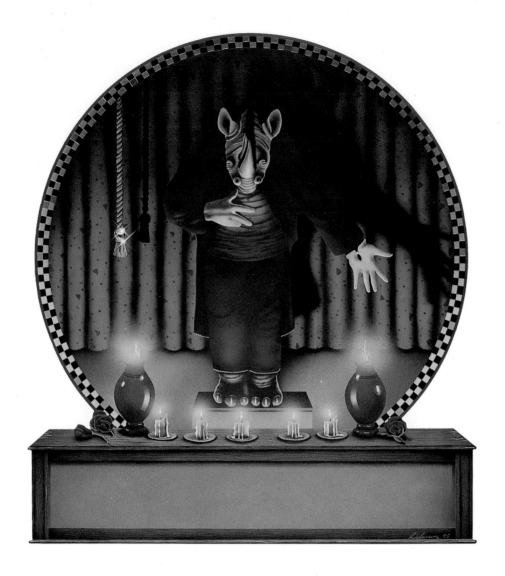

ARTIST'S ACKNOWLEDGEMENTS

Magical Blend, Simon & Schuster, The Unicorn Publishing House, Inc., The Queen's Cards, Inc., Landmark General Publications, The Crossing Press, Harcourt Brace Jovanovich, Buttertoes Gifts, Second Story Books, Stepping Out Arts Magazine,

Maryanne Peterson, Michelle Harris, Asia, Denise Rainear, Seasons Sparks, Cooper Edens, Richard Dix, Shawn Evans, Jackie West, Bill Murry, Russell Kaine, Alan Benjamine, Jean L. Scrocco, Dick Wald, Donna Nelson, Terry and Anneke, Gene Mitchell, Mickey Hart, Jeanne Clemmons, Cindy, Carol, Amy, Lorna, Marilyn and Kate.